TWO MINUTES OF TRADITIONS

Torah and Life Lessons For People on the Go

VOLUME 1

by Rabbi Andrew Bloom

Cover Design by Nava Shoham

TWO MINUTES OF TRADITIONS

ALL RIGHTS RESERVED

Copyright © 2014 Rabbi Andrew Bloom

No part of this publication may be reproduced,
stored in a retrieval system or transmitted or displayed
by any system, in any form, or by any means –
electronic, photocopying, recording or otherwise,
without the prior written permission of the copyright holder,
Who may be contacted at the following address:

Rabbi Andrew Bloom
4050 South Hulen Street
Fort Worth, Texas 76109

Library of Congress Control Number: 2014916632

CreateSpace Independent Publishing Platform, North Charleston, SC

ISBN-13   9781501038366
ISBN-10   1501028367

DEDICATION

To Michal
My Wife, Partner, Best Friend
and the Love of My Life.

You are my inspiration for
all that I do and all that I am.

To Daniel, Maya and Lia
You teach me every day,
through your gentle souls and smiles,
what love is.
I am blessed to be your father.

ACKNOWLEDGEMENTS

Many people have contributed to his book. Most important are the family members, friends, congregants and casual acquaintances I have had the privilege of having as parts of my life.

The Inspiration for my *Facebook, Two Minutes of Torah*, and ultimately this book is due to them and their push for my personal, religious, educational, spiritual and moral quest to bring our sources closer to all who thirst for knowledge encapsulated in just a few paragraphs.

We are such a busy society that I came to realize, Torah and learning needed to be brief and inspirational if it was to be accessible to all.

There are many people that I would like to thank, but they are too numerous to thank individually. Thus I will only mention a few here. However. I want everyone to know that I am thankful to all those who have helped make this book possible.

I would first like to thank my parents who started me out on my Jewish journey through life. Secondly, I would like to thank my mentors who have helped stimulate me as a person and as a Rabbi. They have all had a tremendous impact on me from the time I was a teenager until today.

I especially thank Rabbis Phil Pohl, Andre Ungar, Gary Perras and Sidney Zimelman. Without them I would not be the person or the rabbi that I am today. I would also like to thank all the Cantors with whom I have worked in the past and present for inspiring me musically throughout the years.

My sincerest thanks go out to Larry Steckler whose ideas, hard work, dedication and inspiration have helped make this book possible. He placed within me the fire to turn the electronic teachings of cyberspace into the published words of a book. I am eternally grateful.

My further thanks go out to Joann English, for without her hard work, dedication, guidance and patience this book would not be possible. And I must not forget Louise Vermillion, who became my final proofreader, and Dr. Murray Cohen for writing the introduction to this book.

Additionally, I would like to thank the congregation and congregants that I have had the privilege of serving during the years since I have become a Rabbi, and my sincerest thanks to Congregation Ahavath Sholom in Fort Worth, for being the warmest and most welcoming congregation I have ever had the privilege to be associated with. It is my honor to be part of the CAS family.

I would further like to thank Robert Kaye, who has been a friend, mentor and intellectual stimulator over the past nine years, and whose support has led me to where I am today. I must also thank my best friend and study partner over the past 15 years, Ellis Slater, who has pushed me, taught me, argued with me and expanded my breath of knowledge in so many ways that I will never be able to thank him enough.

To my sister in law, Nava Shoham, one of the most talented artists in our society today, a person who brings Judaism to life through her work, I would like to say thank you for designing this beautiful book cover. It means a lot to me.

To my parents and sister, I want to thank you for being a part of my family and Jewish life. To my children, Daniel, Maya and Lia, you bring joy and light into my life on a daily basis, and the greatest amount of love and no amount of appreciation that I can show will ever be enough thanks for everything you they have afforded me as a father.

Most importantly, I need to thank my wife Michal who is my best friend, partner and the love of my life, as well as being the most patient and loving person in the world. Life has taken us on many paths, but from the first time I saw her, I knew that she was the person that I wanted to spend the rest of my life with. She has given more to our family and me than any one person can give, and all those who know her are better for having such a special person as part of their lives. I love you! This book is for you.

-- Rabbi Andrew Bloom

INTRODUCTION

Modern society demands contemporary interpretation of our ancient texts to enrich our lives, and guide us with the assistance of the wisdom of our Sages.

Meet my Rabbi, Andrew Bloom. As Chair of our shul's Rabbinic Search Committee, I recruited Rabbi Bloom and his beautiful family to the "promised land" of Fort Worth, Texas. I also just completed two years as shul president, working daily with Rabbi Bloom.

Rabbi Andrew Bloom is an extremely talented, energetic, and creative spiritual leader. His methods focus on leadership by example, teaching *Torah* by living *Torah*. His innovations in ministering to our Congregation and indeed our entire Community have made *Torah* lessons an easy yet meaningful daily occurrence that is as easy as checking the weather forecast, or last night's baseball scores. He establishes connections to *Torah* through thoughtful insights, sharing his daily "learning" through social media, and utilizing multiple formats for access to his ideas for all ages.

You are in for a treat with this book! This edition of

some of Rabbi Bloom's daily *"Two Minutes of Torah"* links you with a *Living Torah*. I have found these daily lessons to be akin to taking your Jewish blood pressure, or perhaps stepping on a scale in the morning to get a quick fix on how you are going to approach your day.

Enjoy this book; feel this book; connect with your heritage in an unusually feel-good way; and follow Rabbi Bloom on Facebook and Twitter.

B'Shalom,

Dr. Murray Cohen, President 2012-2014

Congregation Ahavath Sholom, Fort Worth, Texas

CONTENTS

Dedication	2
Acknowledgement	3
Introduction	7
Contents	9
Why This Book?	13
1. Start to the day	19
2. Lecha Dodi and the Sabbath Queen	21
3. The Garden of Eden and the One in our backyard	23
4. Medal of Honor and Honor in Judaism	25
5. Forbes 400 and Who is Rich	26
6. The Week Ahead	28
7. Who is like God?	29
8. From Generation to Generation	30
9. Rain, Rain go Away	32
10. Passover Cleaning	33
11. Allergies in Texas	35
12. Let Freedom Ring	37
13. Jewish Dangers in the Urkraine	39
14. Eeyore or Iyyar?	41
15. More Torah, More Life!	42
16. Praying and Prayer Leaders	44
17. Israel Independence Day	46

18.	How to Live and How to Comfort the Sick	48
19.	Being Insular and Ignoring the Truth	50
20.	Has God's Role in Creation Ended?	52
21.	Mother's Day	54
22.	The Bill of Rights	56
23.	The Gettysburg Address and the Book of Psalms	58
24.	Conflict in Society	60
25.	Mercy or Justice: You Decide!	62
26.	The Shema	64
27.	One's Identity	66
28.	Taking Count of Our Lives	68
29.	Armchair Quarterback	71
30.	Blue Bloods and Birkat Hamazon	73
31.	The Amidah -- Standing Before God	75
32.	Is God's Laughing at us, Good or Bad?	78
33.	Memorial Day	81
34.	God's Dominion	83
35.	Hebrew as the Common Core Language of the Jewish People	85
36.	My Family the Louries or Lurianic Kabbalah?	87
37.	A Person's Name	89
38.	Baby Boys and the Covenant of Circumcision	91
39.	The Neighbor Behind the Fence	93
40.	Revelation, Who, What, When and Where	95
41.	Keeping the Sabbath Holy	97

42. Who's Got the Most Gold? The Golden Rule	100
43. The Letter or the Spirit of the Law; Which is More Important?	102
44. Checkmark Judaism	104
45. Development of Jewish Law	106
46. Halacha	109
47. I'm on Fire: Is the Eternal Light Only in the Temple	112
48. Father's Day	114
49. The Green Head of Jealousy	116
50. Understanding God	118
51. Psalm 30 and our Emotions	120
52. Bubee, Grandma, Mom, and the Next Generations; Connection or Disconnect?	122
53. Schools out? Really?	125
54. Stress in our Lives	128
55. Chosen? Chosen by Whom and What Does this Mean?	131
56. How Do We Pray?	134
57. Psalms for the Day Ahead	137
58. Leaders Who Have Let Us Down	139
59. V'shamru	142
60. Shark Tank and Being Rich	144

PART II
RABBINIC REFLECTIONS

The Theme of Redemption	147
Conformity & Abdication of Independent Thinking	151
Thanksgiving and Pumpkin Pie	156
Development of Beliefs and Torah	161
How Does Israel Blend Independence Day and Memorial Day – One After the Other	166
School's Over!	171
The Sins of our Political Leaders	176
Ellie Wiesel	181
Entering Into a Relationship with God	185
Shabbat Evenings	189
Al Chet and the Sin of Slander	194
Torah, Evolution and Shavout – How Do they All Go Together	198
About the Author	201

WHY THIS BOOK?

To make it possible for you the reader to understand my own personal theology and where I am coming from in relationship to my writing, I would first like to reflect upon four different areas of my own personal belief. These are:

- God
- Free will and man's place in the world
- Revelation
- Kehilah/Community

I will of course begin with the foundation of my individual theology, which is my belief in God. Personally speaking, my belief in God begins with *Genesis 1:1* and then diverges greatly from the classical Jewish view of a proactive God in our world. To be more specific, let me state that I do believe that God created the world and the infinite amount of possibilities that this world holds. However I do not believe that the six days of creation are actually six 24-hour periods of time. For I do not think that creation can be relegated to a fixed amount of hours or days.

Rather I believe that each day describes a stage in the

world's development. Therefore, if we look at each day as a period of development, then I am able to reconcile God's creating the world with the historical evidence of evolution. With this in mind, my belief in God becomes even deeper, for I am able to see the Bible as authentic, as well as accurate, and thus the Bible and God's creation become even more ingrained in my own mind.

I further believe that God put into process through His creations the first step in man's development. To be more precise, I would argue that God placed the *tree of knowledge of good and evil (Genesis 2:17)* purposely and decidedly in the Garden of Eden so that Adam would eat from it. Had man not eaten from the tree then we as a human race would not have developed.

I do not think that God created the world for us to remain in a state of bliss and indifference. However, at this point, I must also state that while I believe God created a multitude of possibilities in our world, I also believe that since then He has ceased to play an active *button pushing* role in the world that we live in.

After mentioning Adam just a few sentences ago, I feel compelled to add that I believe that Adam, and all humankind since Adam, have been and continue to be born in God's image. Man's images are ones of purity and morality leading us to strive towards God, for God is the ultimate representation of truth, which we all try to incorporate into our lives.

Having said that, I must note that there are evil people

in the world who have so totally corrupted and destroyed their own individual images of God that they are no longer capable of good and thus choose to do evil.

This theology is the basis for belief in free will. My view of free will is based on the famous story of *Aknai* that can be found in the *Babylonian Talmud Baba Metzia 59 a-b*.

The story reads; *We learnt elsewhere: If he cut it into separate tiles, placing sand between each tile: R. Eliezer declared it clean, and the Sages declared it unclean; and this was the oven of 'Aknai. Why [the oven of] 'Aknai? — Said Rab Judah in Samuel's name: [It means] that they encompassed it with arguments as a snake, and proved it unclean. It has been taught: On that day R. Eliezer brought forward every imaginable argument, but they did not accept them. Said he to them: "If the halacha agrees with me, let this carob-tree prove it!" Thereupon the carob-tree was torn a hundred cubits out of its place — others affirm, four hundred cubits. "No proof can be brought from a carob-tree," they retorted. Again he said to them: "If the halacha agrees with me, let the stream of water prove it!" Whereupon the stream of water flowed backwards — "No proof can be brought from a stream of water," they rejoined. Again he urged: "If the halacha agrees with me, let the walls of the schoolhouse prove it," whereupon the walls inclined to fall. But R. Joshua rebuked them, saying: "When scholars are engaged in a halachic dispute, what have ye to interfere?" Hence they did not fall, in honour of R. Joshua, nor did they resume the upright, in honour of R. Eliezer; and they are still standing thus inclined. Again he said to them: "If the halacha agrees with me, let it be proved from Heaven!" Whereupon a Heavenly Voice cried out: "Why do ye dispute with R. Eliezer, seeing that in all matters the halacha agrees with him!" But R. Joshua arose and exclaimed: "It is not in heaven." What did he mean by this? — Said R. Jeremiah: That the Torah had already been given at Mount Sinai; we pay no attention to a Heavenly Voice, because Thou hast long since written in the Torah at Mount Sinai, After the majority must one incline.*

R. Nathan met Elijah and asked him: "What did the Holy One, Blessed be He, do in that hour?" — He laughed [with joy], he replied, saying, "My sons have defeated Me, My sons have defeated Me."

This story reinforces my belief that man has free will to act in a way that he believes is correct. Unfortunately some use this free will for evil purposes, but in general I believe that most of us use our free will to do good in the world. It is through this attempt to do good in the world that we become closer to God. God being the holy truth that we try and reach, but can never actually touch.

It is only through our never-ending journey, like that of the angels on the ladder in Jacob's dream that we continue to develop our relationship with God. It is this development of our relationship with God, and with other human beings who are also creations of God whereby we can bring holiness into our lives. Only when we treat both the heavens and the earth, God and man, with respect, honor and love will the image of God that we were born with come out and shine onto others.

As for revelation, I believe that revelation is ongoing. It is our attempt to understand the *Written Torah* and our continuing development of the *Oral Torah* that keep revelation, which began at Mt. Sinai, alive. While the *Tanach* does not change in terms of what has been canonized, our understanding of this canonization is continuously developing. It is in this development that we as human beings keep religion alive, and thus I hope that our own revelation will never cease to exist. I believe that once religion ceases to expand, it will become only a history to be studied and not a tradition that is lived.

This part of my theology is based upon the first *Mishna of Avot: Moses received the Torah at Sinai and transmitted it to Joshua, Joshua to the elders, and the elders to the prophets, and the prophets to the men of the great synagogue. The latter used to say three things; be patient in [the administration of] justice, rear many disciples and make a fence round the Torah. (Avot 1:1)* It is in the chain of tradition and the rearing of many disciples that our revelation continues.

In my own personal theology the component of *Kehila*/community holds a very important place. By *Kehila* I mean all aspects of our communal lives. These include the religious, spiritual, educational and social

17

aspects of our lives as well as many more. For I truly believe what is written in *Sanhedrin 17B* - *It has been taught; A scholar should not reside in a city where any of the following ten things is missing:*

1. *A court of justice*
2. *A charity fund*
3. *A synagogue*
4. *Public baths*
5. *Toilet facilites*
6. *A mohel*
7. *A surgeon*
8. *A notary*
9. *A shohet*
10. *A schoolmaster*

However instead of *A Schoolmaster* my interpretation reads *a kehila*. For if the ten categories listed above are not interpreted literally, but rather in the spirit upon which they were written, *a kehila* implies that that there is a need to fulfill all aspects of a person's life. In my mind this is not only philosophical, but it is also theological and rational as well.

I hope that through understanding who I am and what I believe my writings will encourage you to ponder your own theology and interpretations of my *2 Minutes of Torah* and *Rabbi's Reflections* that are presented in the following chapters.

1. START TO THE DAY

In Jewish tradition we are required to pray three times a day. The first service is based upon the prayers of *Abraham (scharait-morning)*, the second on *Isaac (mincha-afternoon)* and the last on *Jacob (maariv-eveing)*. This obligation connects us to our heritage and places us directly as the descendants of Monotheism and Judaism. There is a prayer that is said during every morning service, which brings focus to the day ahead. I offer it below in the hope that it will bring us closer to God and a good day in front of us.

Should you prefer to adapt this prayer to your own circumstances, please feel free. For our connections to God are not only communal, but also very personal.

Praised are You Adonai our God, who rules the universe, removing sleep from my eyes and slumber from my eyelids. May we feel at home with Your Torah, and cling to Your mitzvoth. Keep us from error, from sin and transgression. Bring us not to trial or to disgrace: let no evil impulse control us. Keep us far from wicked people and corrupt companions. Strengthen our desire to do good deeds; teach us humility, that we may serve You. May we find grace, love, and compassion in Your sight and in the sight of all who look upon us, this day and every day. Grant us a full measure of loving-kindness. Praised are You Adonai, who bestows loving-kindness upon His people.

2. LECHA DODI AND THE SABBATH QUEEN

The prayer *Lecha Dodi* was written by the 16th century kabbalist Rabbi Shlomo HaLevi Alkabetz. For many the beautiful melodies of *Lecha Dodi* are the highlight of the Friday night service where it is traditionally sung. There are eight full stanzas that create an image of the sages greeting the Sabbath.

The practice of welcoming the Sabbath as Israel's bride is mentioned in the *Talmud (Shabbat 119a)* and on the basis of this the sixteenth-century *Kabbalists* in *Safed* developed an elaborate ritual in which they would go out into the fields dressed in white garments to welcome the Sabbath.

Today Jewish congregations around the world usher in the beauty of *Shabbat* and the Sabbath Queen by singing the words of *Lecha Dodi*. Within the prayer the question of Judaic priorities and emphasis can be found. This question being; which is more important, having knowledge of Shabbat (on an intellectual level) or keeping/fulfilling the laws of Shabbat *(Halacha-even if we don't understand why)?*

This discussion has its roots in the 10 commandments where we are once told to *remember (Exodus 20:8)* the

Sabbath and then to *guard (Deuteronomy 5:12)* the Sabbath. To truly sanctify *Shabbat* and enhance our relationship with the community and God, Alkabetz wrote in the first stanza of *Lecha Dodi* that we should *keep and remember in one utterance.* In essence we must both learn the laws and holiness of Shabbat while at the same time keeping *Shabbat's* laws and customs. In the hope that we should be able to do both, I offer a computer link to the prayer below so you can both watch and listen to it.

https://www.youtube.com/watch?v=RWmcQpzUMHY

May God afford us all the opportunity this *Shabbat* to celebrate and welcome in the Sabbath Queen. Enjoy the beautiful version of *Lecha Dodi* from the *Maccabeats* Go to your computer, turn up the volume and watch and listen. It is well worth the time as you will be truly inspired. May God bless us, all *Am Yisrael* and humanity with health, happiness and peace.

3. THE GARDEN OF EDEN AND THE ONE IN OUR BACKYARD

The Garden of Eden was created by God and inhabited by man, for as it is mentioned in the *Book of Genesis, And the LORD God planted a garden in Eden, in the east, and there he put the man whom he had formed (Genesis 2:8)*. The garden itself was paradise on earth for a period of time, until Adam and Eve abused its beauty for their own benefit and not for the betterment and the holiness that God had placed within it.

As we know, gardens benefit from the care and dedication of man as well as the miracles of nature. When the two come together, a garden offers life, sanctuary and inspiration for all those who enter it. *Ezekiel* wrote that *You were in Eden, the garden of God; every precious stone was your covering (Ezekiel 28:13).*

The beauty of his description and what a garden can offer is inspiring. Yesterday, in Fort Worth, the city celebrated an Earth Party. It was a day of respecting and rejuvenating our own Garden of Eden, here in Fort Worth. This celebration is an example of a mitzvah that we should all fulfill not only once a year, but truly on a daily basis.

TWO MINUTES OF TRADITIONS

Congregation Ahavath Sholom, in Fort Worth, has a congregational garden where we tend to the holiness of God, man, community and the beauty of nature. Through the hard work of our dedicated volunteers we were able to donate over 900 pounds of vegetables to our local Food Bank and Jewish Family Services last year.

Gan Ahavath Sholom incorporates that which we are taught in the Book of Deuteronomy *God upholds the cause of the orphan and the widow, and befriends the stranger, providing him/her with food and clothing. -- You too must befriend the stranger, for you were strangers in the land of Egypt. (Deuteronomy 10:18-19)*

While we no longer live in the Garden of Eden that God created for Adam and Eve, we can grow one that gives life to ourselves, our community and respect to God. May every day be an Earth Day and celebration of life for us, all *Am Yisrael* and humanity.

4. MEDAL OF HONOR AND HONOR IN JUDAISM

The Congressional Medal of Honor is awarded to soldiers who have shown exemplary bravery and honor during war and combat operations. I salute not only them, but all soldiers who have served and are presently serving in the armed forces of the United States, Israel and all other democratic and free countries.

Honor is not just a value that can be found on the battlefield, for it can also be worn as a badge of pride by all who embrace the values held within this world. The question is; how do we find honor in our lives, and what does it mean?

For the answer to this, I look towards *Pirkei Avot (Ethics of the Fathers) Chapter 4 Mishnah 1,* where we read: *Who is honored? Those who honor all people; as it is written; "Those who honor Me (God), I will honor. But those who scorn Me will be despised" (Samuel 2:3).* Let us remember that the badge of honor that we can earn is through *honoring all people* and although this badge might not be presented by the President of the United States at the White House (as the Congressional Medal of Honor is), it is presented by God and is something that we can probably attain.

5. FORBES 400 AND WHO IS RICH

Each year, *Forbes Magazine* puts out a list of the richest individuals in the world, called the *Billionaires List*. This year's edition of the list came out in the last two months. Names such as Bill Gates, Warren Buffet, Mark Cuban, and Jerry Jones are only a few of those who are mentioned. We wish them and all others on this list God's continued health and inspiration, so that they can continue to use their fortunes in helping out those in need, and humanity as a whole.

However, *Forbes Magazine,* does not provide the only list of those who are rich, for in *Pirkei Avoth (Ethics of the Fathers)* we can find another list of all those who are wealthy. In *Chapter 4 Mishnah 1, we read Who is rich? One who is satisfied with his lot. As is stated (Psalms 128:2): If you eat of toil of your hands, fortunate are you, and good is to you; fortunate are you in this world, and good is to you in the World to Come.*

The author of this *mishnah*, Ben Zoma, lays out a path whereby each and every one of us, irrespective of our monetary wealth can find richness; richness within our souls and satisfaction with the blessings that God has bestowed upon us.

Thus according to *Pirkei Avoth,* the list of the rich is open to all who strive towards it. It is my hope, that we as a community both near and far will find the richness within us, and the blessings that God offers us. If we are able to accomplish this, then the true list of the rich will include all of our names.

6. THE WEEK AHEAD

Shavuah Tov. Let me begin by wishing everyone a blessed week ahead. There are times, usually on *Shabbat* afternoon that I find myself pondering if the week ahead will be one filled with confidence or fright? Will the week bring me, my family and those around me blessings or frustrations?

These sorts of thoughts can be pretty heavy and scary at times. It is at these moments that I understand the beauty and importance of the opening words of the *havdalah* service that is recited at the conclusion of *Shabbat*. They say *Behold, God is my deliverance; I am confident and unafraid. Adonai is my strength, my might, my deliverance; with joy shall you draw water from the wells of deliverance (First Paragraph of Havdalah).* It is almost as if these opening verses, which are drawn from Isaiah, Psalms and Esther, are impressing upon me that the week ahead will be one filled with blessings, that God is with me, and that there is nothing to be afraid of. When I recited these words at the close of this week's *Shabbat*, it was with the hope and prayer that God should fulfill these words for each and every one of us. May God bless us all during the upcoming week with health and happiness.

7. WHO IS LIKE GOD?

During morning services in the paragraph leading up to the famous words, and song *Mi Chamocha (Who is like You, Adonai, among all that is worshiped…)*, we read the words *happy is he who listens to your commandments and Your Torah and places Your words in his heart.*

It would seem that these words serve as a roadmap to answering the question *Who is like you Adonai?* The answer is that nothing on earth or in the heavens is equal to God. Thus to enter into a deep covenantal relationship with God we must *put His Torah in our hearts* and consequently we can live as the *happy person* that the verse opens up with.

It is my hope and prayer that we should use our time today, to study and pray, so that God will enter our hearts and we will find the deep happiness of life that we all are looking for. Enjoy your day.

8. FROM GENERATION TO GENERATION

Let me first wish everyone a *Shabbat Shalom* and a terrific weekend. May God bless us, and our families with peace, holiness, love and *mitzvoth*. During this upcoming *Shabbat* we will be celebrating at the synagogue a number of joyous events.

Friday night, during services, our K-1 Hebrew School students will be participating and leading parts of our services. Saturday morning our 8th graders will be reading from the *Torah*, and leading us in *davening*. We are taught *L'Dor V'Dor (From generation to generation)*, and this *Shabbat* the saying will truly be coming to fruition.

Furthermore, during *Shabbat* morning services we will be celebrating with a processional directly before the *Torah* service, the dedication of our new Torah Covers. We sing the words in front of the ark *It is a tree of life for all those who grasp onto it (Proverbs 3:18)* and we invite the entire community to come and grasp onto the *Tree of Torah* during this dedication.

We conclude both services with the words *Adon Olam (master of the universe),* which is a very meaningful and beautiful prayer that emphasizes the belief of God being timeless, infinite and omnipotent. Below, you will find a link to a version of *Adon Olam* sung by an IDF band that is performed for soldiers all across Israel. I remember them coming out to my base to entertain our unit in between combat deployments and enjoying their performance very much. I hope you do as well.

Sit down in front of your computer, type in the link, turn up the volume and enjoy.

https://www.youtube.com/watch?v=VmFCmvMnFJA&list=PL9AE180962EEE5DEB

9. RAIN, RAIN, GO AWAY

Good morning. It is thundering and raining outside and many of us have awakened to a wet day ahead. For some of us this means changing our plans for today. However, instead of seeing the rain as an inconvenience, Judaism teaches us that *when rain falls it is as great as the day on which heaven and earth were created (Babylonian Talmud, Ta'anit 8a)*.

Furthermore, we are taught that if we act with a pure heart and follow God's statues that; *I will send you rain in its season, and the ground will yield its crops and the trees their fruit. Your threshing will continue until grape harvest and the grape harvest will continue until planting, and you will eat all the food you want and live in safety in your land (Leviticus 26:4-6).*

So let us follow the message of our sources, and instead of changing our plans and complaining about having to do so, let us embrace our *mitzvoth* and thus bring even more of this much needed rain to our cities and State, as well as God's blessings upon us. Enjoy your day, and the blessings that the rain brings with it.

10. PASSOVER CLEANING

It's started! I don't mean the countdown to tonight's NCAA championship game between Kentucky and Connecticut; rather I am referring to *Passover cleaning*. When I mention the words, *Passover cleaning*, one immediately gets the chills and associates this with the cleaning of the house. However, there is another sort of cleaning, the cleansing of one's soul. I am referring here to the cleansing of our bad habits, our shortcomings and often our moral outlooks (on any number of ideas or situations).

Therefore, the question that follows is: What path should one pursue to cleanse our souls? I believe the answer to this question can be found in *Pirkei Avot 2:13 (Ethics of the Fathers)*, where we find the following mishna.

He posed this question to his disciples; Look about you and tell me-which is the way in life to which one should cleave? Rabbi Eliezer said: A generous eye; Rabbi Y'hoshua said: A good colleague; Rabbi Yose said: A good neighbor; Rabbi Shimon said: Foresight; Rabbi Elazar said: A generous heart. Said he to them; I prefer the answer of Elazar ben Arakh, for his view includes all of yours.

As we can conclude from this *mishna*, the path towards Passover soul cleansing follows the teaching of having a *generous heart*. May God grant us all the strength to follow this path, and thus have a truly kosher Passover.

11. ALERGIES IN TEXAS

One thing that I have noticed since moving to Texas three years ago, is that we appear to be the allergy center of the world. If I don't see at least ten people rubbing their eyes or sneezing each day, than my day is not complete, and this includes me. Claritin anyone? Can't we fix the world, or at least change the allergy season to only a few brief weeks? I don't know about a few brief weeks, but even a few brief months would be OK with me.

While I am sure that many of us would like to change the creation of the world so it would no longer include allergies, I am reminded of the following *midrash*. *When God created the first human beings, God led them around the garden of Eden and said: 'Look at my works! See how beautiful they are -- how excellent! For your sake I created them all. See to it that you do not spoil and destroy My world; for if you do, there will be no one else to repair it.' (Midrash Kohelet Rabbah, 1 on Ecclesiastes 7:13).*

In essence, the *midrash* is telling us, that although the world may be imperfect in our eyes, it is God's creation and we must protect it. While fewer allergies might be nice, the complex order of the world, reminds us that one inconvenience in the larger blessings of creation is not a reason to complain or want to change the world. I hope that even though our eyes might be watering at this time of the year, we can still appreciate the beauty around us.

12. LET FREEDOM RING

I hope everyone enjoyed their *seders*, and that the message of freedom still resonates within each of us. There was an Iraqi folktale called *From Rags to Riches*, that we read at our family *seder* this year. While our *haggadahs* may be put away until next year, I believe that the lessons of this folktale are appropriate for our daily lives. For Judaism is transferable and not specific for any one date or event.

The folktale relates; That when the old king died, a bird called the 'bird of good fortune' would be released. On whosoever head it landed, the people would place the crown making him their next ruler.

Once the bird of good fortune landed on the head of a slave. That slave had been a simple musician who entertained at the master's parties. His costume consisted of a feathered cap, and a belt made of the hooves of sheep. When the slave became king, he moved into the palace and wore royal robes.

However, he ordered that a shack be constructed next to the palace and that his old hat, belt and drum be stored there along with a giant mirror. The new king was known for his kindness and love for all his people- rich and poor, free and slave.

Often he would disappear into his little shack. Once he left its door open and the cabinet ministers saw him don his feathered hat, put on his old belt and dance and drum before the mirror. They found this very strange and asked the king; 'after all, you are a king! You must maintain your dignity!' The king replied;

'Once I was a slave and now I've become a king. From time to time I want to remind myself that I was once a slave, lest I grow arrogant and treat with disdain my people and you, my ministers.'

Without doubt a lesson well worth learning.

13. JEWISH DANGERS IN THE UKRAINE

After the German invasion of Poland in 1939, Jews were made to wear a yellow Star of David badge. On September 19, 1941, Reinhard Heydrich signed a decree making the wearing of the yellow Star of David badge mandatory for all Jews living in territory under Nazi control.

We all know the rest of the story, six-million murdered and future generations of families lost. However, what we might not know is that another attempt to register Jews is ongoing today and taking place in the Ukraine. George Santayana (December 16, 1863 – September 26, 1952) once was quoted as saying *Those who cannot remember the past are condemned to repeat it (Reason in Common Sense-1905)*.

Are we in the midst of repeating history? I hope not. But if we ignore the reality that our Jewish brethren are suffering and being persecuted in the Ukraine at this time, then we will also be to blame for them becoming the scapegoat of unrest in the area. It is now time for us to make our voices heard.

I will be sending a letter of concern for, and in support of, the Ukrainian Jewish community to our local, state and national politicians, and I hope that you will join me in protesting and having our voices heard.

Should you like to add your name to this letter, please contact the synagogue office as soon as possible (Congregation Ahavath Sholom, via our website at www.ahavathsholom.org), and let us know that you stand with us in support of the Jewish Community in Ukraine.

14. EEYORE OR IYYAR?

Beginning last night (Tuesday), and continuing today (Wednesday), and tomorrow (Thursday), Jews around the world, will celebrate the New Month of *Iyyar*. During the *Shabbat* service preceding the new month, it is traditional after the *haftorah* has been chanted, and before the *Torah* has been returned to the ark, to announce the upcoming new month.

Within the prayer that is chanted, we recite the words; *May it be Your will, Lord our God and God of our ancestors, to renew our lives in the coming month. Grant us a long life, a peaceful life, with goodness and blessing,, sustenance and physical vitality, a life formed by purity and piety, a life free from shame and reproach, a life of abundance and honor, a life embracing piety and love of Torah, a life in which our heart's desires for goodness will be fulfilled. Amen (Siddur Sim Shalom For Shabbat and Festivals-Published Rabbinical Assembly 1985 page 419).*

May the words of the prayer come to fruition in our lives. *Hodesh Tov (A good month)!*

15. MORE TORAH. MORE LIFE!

In *Pirkei Avot* we read *More Torah, More Life (Pirkei Avot 2:8)*. The question arises as to the origin of this saying. How do we know that more *Torah* brings about more life?

When such a question comes to the forefront of a discussion, the first place to search is, logically, in a more ancient text. In all textual cases in Judaism, the original sources that need to be consulted can be found in the *Torah*. In the *Book of Deuteronomy we read; When he is seated on his royal throne, he shall have a copy of this Torah written for him on a scroll by the levitical priests. And it will be with him and he will read it all the days of his life, so that he will learn to revere the Lord his God, to faithfully observe every word of this Torah and these laws (Deuteronomy 17:18-19).*

In essence, these verses are relating to us that no matter what the status of an individual in life may be, the *Torah* should always serve as his/her source of *life*. This equality of responsibility for *Torah* learning, shows us that we are all liable in furthering God's teachings, both in our daily lives and at the same time, within the wider community.

TWO MINUTES OF TRADITIONS

I hope through our mutual learning, that we will all serve as conduits to God's words becoming even more central to the society that we live in.

***Today is my grandmother's *yahrtzeit,* and I dedicate these words of *Torah*, to the *Torah* that she taught me, through how she lived her life.

16. PRAYING AND PRAYER LEADERS

I have had the privilege of *davening* (praying) in synagogues around the world. In Jerusalem, I was able to pray in a small synagogue near our home that was no larger than a 10 by 14-foot room. While in England, I was able to *daven* in an old English Synagogue near Abbey Road (no I didn't see Ringo Starr), and through USY on Wheels and my family's travels throughout the United States, I have prayed in *shuls* in more than 30 states.

What strikes me at each synagogue -- no matter if the service is during the week, on *Shabbat* or on a holiday -- is the wide variety of prayer leaders that can be found leading services. However, no matter where I may be *davening,* there is always one thing that remains common to all synagogues, and that is, the *kavannah (intention)* of the *shaliach tzibur (public prayer leader).*

Considering all of my experiences, I began to wonder, how does a community choose its prayer leaders? Is it due to someone's voice, knowledge, family heritage, or possibly a combination of all these and more? The answer for each synagogue varies, but the *Shulha Aruch (Code of Jewish Law authored by Josef Karo in*

1563) offers us a hint.

In Karo's work, we find the following passage; *The shaliah tzibbur must be of good character. What is good character? That the person is free of sins and does not have a bad reputation (even in his youth), is humble, acceptable to the people, possessing a pleasant voice, and accustomed to chanting biblical selections (Shulhan Aruch, Orah Hayyim 53:4).*

As we can see, simply having a good voice, or volunteering to lead a service is not enough. Rather, the entirety of a person's character must be on a level where he or she can represent the congregation's prayers before God, and bring God's word back down to the congregation. Without doubt, a tall order to fulfill, but a fulfilling one when accomplished.

I hope that the prayers of this *Shabbat* will inspire us to lead a life like that of a *shaliach tzibbur*. For even if we are not the one leading services, who knows, one day we might be asked, and wouldn't it be nice to have all the characteristics mentioned by Karo. Thus we would be able to speak with God, and be spoken to by God as well.

May this *Shabbat* bring our voices closer to God and His closer to us. Let me take this opportunity to wish all of us, our families and the entire nation of *Am Yisrael*, a *Shabbat Shalom*. May it be filled with moments of peace, family, community and spirituality.

17. ISRAEL INDEPENDENCE DAY

Zionist synagogues throughout the world, during services this morning, chanted a special *Torah* reading in honor of Israel Independence Day. The reading itself is taken from *parshat Ekev,* and more specifically, *Deuteronomy 7:12-8:18.*

Within the morning's reading, the following verse which is read, is quite appropriate; *You shall faithfully observe all the Instruction that I enjoin upon you today, that you may thrive and increase and be able to possess the land that the Lord promised on oath to your fathers' (Deuteronomy 8:1).*

The words *you may increase,* can be understood as, a promise that the Israelites will possess the entire Land of Israel. What does this mean? It is a promise that the character, culture, religion and sovereignty of Israel will always remain under the control of the descendants of King David, in other words, the Jewish people.

Today, just as during the Biblical period of Moses, Joshua and their descendants, it is incumbent upon both God and ourselves to ensure that the Biblical prophecy of a Jewish nation in Israel remains not only a reality, but even more so, a thriving growing, free and independent nation. I hope and pray that this lesson, will not only go viral, but also be taken deeply to heart.

May God bless the State of Israel, and the people of Israel, now and forever more! *Am Israel Chai (The Nation/People* of Israel are alive)!

18. HOW TO LIVE AND HOW TO COMFORT THE SICK

Unfortunately throughout life, we have all had to deal with illness, either of ourselves, our families or friends. Occasionally, we have even had to visit loved ones dying in the hospital, however we still go. Is there another reason that we face head on, the reality of human frailty at its gravest of moments?

Of course love and respect for our families and friends play a large part in the equation. However, I believe that there is something more. Judaism places the ultimate emphasis on life. *Pikuach Nefesh (saving a life)* is one of the definitive values in Judaism. As a matter of a fact it overrides all *mitzvoth* and *halacha* except for the three cardinal sins within Judaism -- murder, immoral sexual relations and idol worship.

This still does not answer the question of; where does the obligation to visit the sick come from. The answer can be found in a Talmudic story written in *The Book of Legends,* for there we read; *One of Rabbi Akiva's disciples fell ill, and the sages did not come to visit him. So Rabbi Akiva went to visit the disciple and because he saw to it that the ground was swept and sprinkled for him, he recovered and said, "My master you have brought me back to life!" Rabbi Akiva went out and expounded, "He who does not visit the sick is as though he sheds blood" (The Book of Legends, The Deeds of Sages P.236:168).*

As we can see, Judaism has given us the foundations of not only how to live, but also how, through visiting the sick, we give others the opportunity of embracing life. Our visits may not heal a person physically; however, what they will do, is help a person feel the dignity of life, even when he is at the darkest of moments. I hope that both our inner self, and the outer teachings of Judaism, will afford us the knowledge that we need to look after all of God's peoples, and not only those who are healthy. In essence those who are suffering need us the most.

19. BEING INSULAR AND IGNORING THE TRUTH

Human beings are very insular in their core beings. We want to live among others who think as we do, whose moral values are close to ours, and whose religious/educational foundations are similar to our own. It is natural for individuals to want to be part of a group, and thus we often gravitate to people we feel most comfortable with.

This self-identification can become problematic, when one group believes that they hold the ultimate truth, and excludes everyone else who does not believe as they do. In terms of Biblical and Rabbinic Judaism, we have learned that the development of ideas, commentary and values is an ever evolving and living organism.

As a matter of fact, *Maimonides*, wrote; *And take note: the things I say in these chapters...are not new concepts that I have invented. They are an anthology from our sages...and the works of philosophers...Hear the truth from whoever said it (Eight Chapters of the Rambam: Introduction)*. *Maimonides* was attempting to teach us that no one group holds the singular and ultimate truth, and learning that is limited to one viewpoint, is in essence, lacking.

TWO MINUTES OF TRADITIONS

The basis of education, is the free flow of ideas and norms, based upon validity and morality and not on self-defining groups and their opinions. We here in modern society, and within the traditional Jewish world, need to understand that only when we bring commentary and community, *midrash* and modernity and self-identity with community together, will we have the opportunity not only to learn from each other, but even more important to live side by side with each other.

Should we succeed in this endeavor, than the world we live in will not only support one's personal preferences, but will also support society's pluralistic personality. I hope that we can learn from the *Rambam* and help bring the type of society that *Maiminides* wrote about into our communities and lives.

20. HAS GOD'S ROLE IN CREATION ENDED?

This evening, as we do every Friday night, Jews around the world will welcome *Shabbat* with prayers, songs and praise. One of the most beautiful prayers that is sung after the *Ma'ariv amidah is, Vay'chulu.*

The prayer itself, is in actuality, a quote from the *Book of Genesis,* and there we read; *The heavens and the earth, and all they contain, were completed. On the seventh day God finished the work He had been doing, and ceased on the seventh day from all the work that He had done. Then, God blessed the seventh day and called it holy, because on it God ceased from all the work of creation (Genesis 2:1-3).*

The question that arises from this quote can be seen in both a philosophical and theological manner. That question is; has creation ceased, or has only God's initial creation of the world ended?

If we were to believe that the world has already been created in its final form on the sixth day of creation, then we could be led to believe that all events both past and present, are out of our control, and thus, why should we attempt through *Tikkun Olam (the value of repairing the world)* to make it better? On the other hand, if only God's role in creation ended on the sixth day, and from then on it fell into our hands to take up the mantle of steering evolution; then through our own efforts we could make the world a better place to live in.

Consequently, we would all share in the responsibility of using our unique God given talents and gifts, to move the ball of creation forward to its next logical point; one of compromise and cooperation, instead of arguments and destruction.

I pray that during the hours of *Shabbat*, we can ponder the words within the *Vay'chulu*, and not only celebrate God's creations, but also help to ensure their positive evolution.

Here is a link to a video of *Varda Noga Spielman* singing *Vay'chulu*. You can watch and listen to it on your computer.

https://www.youtube.com/watch?v=RBmBvRZMTT0

I hope it will inspire your prayers and bring inspiration to your *Shabbat*.

21. MOTHER'S DAY

In Judaism, women have always played a central role in the development of society and the shaping of our communities. In the *Book of Genesis* we read; *Then the Lord God formed a man from the dust of the ground and breathed into his nostrils the breath of life, and the man became a living being (Genesis 2:7).*

From this verse, we can conclude that God *formed* man. However, when we look at the creation of woman, we read something completely different. For there it is written that; *Then the Lord God built a woman from the rib He had taken out of the man, and he brought her to the man (Genesis 2:22).*

From the use of the word *built* instead of *formed*, traditional commentators believed that women were born with a greater degree of intuition, understanding and intelligence than men. They came to this conclusion when they compared the root of the world *built* to the root of the word *binah* (intelligence) in Hebrew *(Bet, Nun, Hey)*. Seeing how the root of both these words were the same, the commentators came to the conclusion that the status of women should be held in the highest esteem.

It is this example of honor and esteem that we should hold up when we thank our mothers, wives and all the other important women in our lives on a day like today. In actuality, it is with this sort of respect and esteem that we should treat the important people in our lives every day. Let me wish all the mothers, both near and far, a happy Mother's Day. May God continue to bless you with the love of your families and the esteem of all those around you.

22. THE BILL OF RIGHTS

The United States of America was founded upon the belief of religious freedom. In the Bill of Rights (the collective name for the first 10 amendments of the American Constitution), which came into effect as Constitutional Amendments on December 15, 1791, we read; *Congress shall make no law respecting an establishment of religion, or prohibiting the free exercise thereof; or abridging the freedom of speech, or of the press; or the right of the people to assemble, and to petition the government for a redress of grievances.*

As we can see from this statement, liberty is at the core of the democracy that we live in. However, this statement is only 223 years old. If we were to go back in time, over 2500 years ago, we would find this same sentiment in an even more central Bill of Rights, and that is in the center of the *Torah*. In the *Book of Leviticus,* we read; *Proclaim liberty throughout the land, for all of its inhabitants (Leviticus 25:10).*

Here the author of Leviticus (God or Man -- you make your own determination) is trying to impart upon the Biblical generation and those to follow, the message that God's image is within each and every one of us, and thus we must ensure that there will always be *liberty throughout the land* for all.

It is my hope and prayer that we who live here in the United States, and those who look to us as a beacon of freedom, can remember not only the words of our Constitution but also the words of our *Torah*; for together they are the foundations of all that is good in this world.

23. THE GETTYSBURG ADDRESS AND THE BOOK OF PSALMS

I love history, especially presidential history, and while I was watching the movie Lincoln, with Daniel Day Lewis playing the part of Abraham Lincoln, the other evening, I was reminded of his words within the Gettysburg address.

The Gettysburg address itself, which is one of the most famous speeches in all of American history, was recited on November 19, 1863, at the dedication of the Soldiers National Cemetery in Gettysburg, Pennsylvania. In his speech, Lincoln spoke the following words; *We here highly resolve that these dead shall not have died in vain, that this nation under God, shall have a new birth of freedom, and that government of the people, by the people, and for the people shall not perish from the earth (Abraham Lincoln-Gettysburg Address).*

These famous words, which always bring chills to my spine, remind me of the writings we find in the *Book of Psalms,* for in that book we read; *How good and how pleasant it is when brethren live in unity (Psalm 133:1).*

TWO MINUTES OF TRADITIONS

The *Book of Psalms*, like the Gettysburg Address, is trying to teach us, that even when one has been in conflict with another, the period that immediately follows it needs to be used for healing and unity.

Today's world is filled with conflict and war, and I hope that through the reminder of Lincoln's legacy and the writings of the *Psalmist*, that we will be able to change this path, and work towards the unity that all of us so dearly yearn for.

24. CONFLICT IN SOCIETY

As we look around us, we are witnesses to conflict within all spheres of society. We see family conflict, communal discord, sectarian violence, national and international jealousies and viciousness in all manner of issues. This is the sad truth of our society, and we call it human reality.

However, if we were to look at *Pirkei Avot (Ethics of the Fathers)*, we would see that society, even with all of its differences, can succeed if the following recipe is followed; *Every assembly whose purpose is to serve God will in the end be established; but every assembly whose purpose is not for God's sake, will not in the end be established (Pirkei Avoth 4:14).*

Unfortunately, disagreements and violence today, are not for the sake of God (for would God truly want murder and genocide among His creations?), but rather for our own selfish reasons. Thus, while it is natural for people to disagree and debate (Judaism believes in and supports pluralism and discussion), we should try and accomplish these disagreements within the realm of making the world a better place, instead of merely trying to conquer the other so we can raise our own station in life.

TWO MINUTES OF TRADITIONS

In my view, it is natural to have beliefs and opinions, but these should never come at the price of others having to lose those same freedoms that we hold so close to our hearts.

25. MERCY OR JUSTICE: YOU DECIDE

Is having mercy upon another, specifically speaking, when the other doesn't necessarily deserve it, a value that we should hold, or is *an eye for an eye and a tooth for a tooth (Exodus 21:24)* the path that needs to be taken?

I believe that the answer to this varies due to circumstances, especially if we study *Exodus 21:24* as referring to economical compensation for damages done to another human being. This position can be seen in *The Babylonian Talmud* where it says; *R. Shimon bar Yohai stated: Eye for eye – money. You say money, but perhaps it means literally an eye? In that case if a blind man blinded another, a cripple maimed another, how would I be able to give an eye for an eye literally? Yet the Torah states (Lev. 24:22): One law there shall be for you – a law that is equitable for all of you. In other circumstances, mercy (or second chances) is also a path to follow (Baba Kama 83b-84a).*

On the other hand, if we were to look at the second path, we could find the reason for mercy in *Maimonides, Laws Pertaining to Acquisition,* for there we read; *And similarly, with regard to the attributes of the Holy One, blessed be He, which He commanded us to emulate, it is written: His mercies upon all His works (Psalms 145:9). And whoever shows mercy to others will have mercy shown to him, as implied by Deuteronomy 13:18: He will show you mercy, and be merciful upon you and multiply you. (Maimonides, Laws of Acquisition 9:8).*

As we can see, Judaism demands justice and mercy, compassion and compensation, responsibility and understanding. It is this type of society that God created; not one that allows for total mercy or total strict judgment and it is this sort of society that we should live in. I hope that the calls that we see on the TV and in the newspaper for only one kind of justice (on both sides) will realize that only a balanced judiciary as Judaism suggests will help perpetuate society, instead of tearing it down along lines of ideology and partisanship.

26. THE SHEMA

The *Shema*, which we pray both in the morning and the evening, is one of the most well-known religious and liturgical prayers in Judaism. The *Shema* was recited publicly after the Decalogue in the Temple service, and by the first century C.E. the three paragraphs *(Deut. 6: 4-9, Deut. 11: 13-21, Num. 15:39)* that formulate it became the centerpiece of Jewish prayer alongside the *Amidah*.

The very first paragraph of the *Shema* alone can be interpreted on four different levels.

1. *...The Lord is One* -- speaks about the unity of God and Judaism's belief in monotheism.
2. *And you shall love...* -- speaks to us on an emotional (love) level.
3. *And you shall teach them...* -- speaks to ones intellect.
4. *And you shall bind them...* -- speaks to the ritual side of Judaism.

As we can see the *Shema* speaks to our emotions and intellect, while at the same time being both covenantal and cultural within the lives of the Jewish people. This prayer is truly a multi-faceted and deeply rich prayer, and one of the paths through which Jews throughout the ages have always connected to *Adonai*.

Rabbi Max Arzt, former Vice Chancellor of the Jewish Theological Seminary, once wrote, that *only when all four of these aspects come together in one's life can he/she truly embrace Judaism in general and God in specific (Max Arzt, Justice and Mercy, New York: The Burning Bush Press, 1963. pg.69-70).*

In this light we can understand that learning to pray takes many different forms and needs to be addressed on many different levels. However, the main component of spiritual growth is, in fact, the opportunity to discover multiple paths toward finding meaning in our daily prayer lives.

I hope that this realization, and the knowledge of the different levels of meaning within the *Shema*, will help us all deepen our prayer lives.

27. ONE'S IDENTITY

Shavuah Tov and good morning. I hope that everyone had a restful and meaningful *Shabbat*. During this past week, while attending a Rabbinical Assembly Convention in Dallas, the question of an individual's Jewish identity, and the importance of guarding this identity came up often in discussions.

While contemplating this question over *shabbat*, a *midrash* from *Genesis Rabbah,* came to mind. The *midrash* asks the question of *why is Abraham called a Hebrew? (Genesis 14:13).*

The *Midrash* notes, that the root of *ivri*, the word for *Hebrew,* can mean either *Hebrew*, or *side*, as in the side of a river *(Genesis Rabbah 42:8).* Based on that interpretation, the *midras*h states, *Abraham was on one side of the river, and the rest of the world was on the other.*

Being on one side of the river, when the rest of our society is on the other (without actually cutting ourselves off from the other side) can actually be the very essence of Jewish survival. After more than a century of fighting our way into the center of society, the next big question that looms ahead for American Jews is whether we will have the courage to proudly stand up for our own identity, no matter what side of the river this might place us on.

I believe that the path we should follow is one where we celebrate who we are, and not shy away from proudly identifying ourselves with the Jewish community. The *Torah* teaches us to be, *a light among the nations (Isaiah 49:6)*. To accomplish this we need to be proud of our religion, our history, our heritage, our beliefs and our individuality.

I hope that the discussions of Jewish identity through hard work, pride and Torah education, will be one not centered around how do we *keep our identity,* but rather on how we have *strengthened* our identity.

I look forward to travelling this path with everyone. May God bring blessings to us all during the week ahead.

28. TAKING COUNT OF OUR LIVES

In this week's *parsha, BaMidbar*, which begins the fourth book of the *Torah,* we read that God commands Moses to *take a census of the whole Israelite community by the clans of its ancestral house (Numbers 1:2).*

There are a number of different explanations as to why there was a need for a census. The most traditional explanation is so that the Israelites would know how many men there were that were eligible for military conscription.

Additionally, there is also a *Midrash* that compares God to a person with precious jewels. This *midrash* goes on to say that such a person is like a jewel who every once in a while is taken out and enjoyed *(Bamidbar Rabbah 4:2).*

A further interpretation can be found in the words of the *Rambam*, who wrote that the census was an important historical lesson. It came to show the Israelites themselves and the nations around them that they have survived in spite of being persecuted and attacked.

Finally, there is an important textual understanding written by Levi Yitzhak of Berdichev. Berdichev, connects the final total of *603,550 (Numbers 1:46)* to a tradition that there are 603,550 letters in the Torah. He reasons that just as the absence of one letter renders a Torah scroll unfit for use, the loss of even one Jew prevents Israel from fulfilling its divine mission.

In my mind, what Berdichev was referring to was the loss of a member within *Klal Yisrael (the entire People of Israel)*. Here we see that while the individual is important, only a *minyan (the community that comes together)* of ten, allows us to read *Torah* publicly. This shows us that the individual must also be part of the whole.

Each and every one of us has a name (our personal names and stories) which should be valued and cherished. But communally we have another name, that being, the *People of Israel*. This is what Berdichev was talking about; togetherness and community.

Today we are much greater in numbers than the census taken in this week's *parsha*, thus the question that needs to be asked is; do we still need to worry about losing Jews?

The answer to this question is, Yes!

We are losing Jews to assimilation, lack of education, indifference, diluting of our religious beliefs.

Therefore, in my mind, we must listen to Berdichev even today.

Even the loss of one member of *Klal Yisrael* dilutes our future. We must take a different sort of census today, being, a census of our values, our communities, our beliefs and ourselves, if we are to survive in the millennia to come. For as we read in the *Ethics of the Fathers, if not now, when (PIrkei Avot 1:15).*

29. ARMCHAIR QUARTERBACK

I was watching Sport Center on ESPN last night, and there was a report that spoke about how veteran quarterbacks often don't hand the reins of the team over to the rookies with ease and grace. Of course, Johnny Manziel's name came into the discussion, as did another quarterback who slid in a past draft, Aaron Rodgers of the Green Bay Packers.

Historically, we know that Brett Favre did not want to hand over the team to Aaron Rodgers, just as Brian Hoyer might oppose Johnny Manziel taking any snaps. When pondering the cutthroat nature of sports, I started to think about how Judaism deals with transitions. The starkest example of this would be the transition from Moses to Joshua.

In the *Book of Numbers*, Moses after being told earlier that he will not enter the Land of Israel, asks God for a second chance. God responds to Moses' heartfelt request in the following manner: *Single out Joshua son of Nun, an inspired man.... Invest him with some of your authority so that the whole Israelite community may obey (Numbers 27:18-20).*

God would not allow Moses to enter the Promised

Land; rather He wanted Moses to show the people that Joshua was also Moses' choice to lead the community. The orderly and enthusiastic passing on of authority was a great gift to Joshua, endowing him with credibility in the eyes of the people, who probably dreaded the death of Moses even more than Moses himself did.

Had Brett Favre understood this, then maybe he would be remembered in even higher esteem than he already is in Green Bay, for he would have been seen as someone who brought success to the team in the past, and helped to guarantee its continued success in the future.

As to my other football example, while I am in no way a Browns or Johnny Manziel fan, I do think that all sports teams could learn from Judaism's example on how we navigate the transitions that we all go through, both on and off the field. Successfully navigating the issues that transitions bring will allow us all to be successful no matter where we are in the depth chart of life.

30. BLUE BLOODS AND BIRKAT HAMAZON

I often tape the show *Blue Bloods* and watch it on my day off as I am a sucker for police and family dramas. During each episode, the Reagan family sits around the table for their Sunday dinner, and says grace before the meal.

In Judaism, the thanking of God *(Birkat Hamazon)*, takes place after; not before the meal. The commandment to give thanks to God, can be found in the *Book of Deuteronomy;* the verse reads, *When you have eaten your fill, give thanks to Adonai your God for the good land that God has given you (Deuteronomy 8:10)*.

These thanks/blessings praise God for creation, express gratitude for the land of Israel, for redemption, the *Covenant*, and the *Torah*. They further request God's mercy and the restoration of Israel, while at the same time asking for the fulfillment of specific desires, in consortium with expressing gratitude for God's goodness *(Themes can be found in the Babylonian Talmud, Berachot 48b)*. Specifically speaking, these blessings and themes can be broken up into four distinct portions within the *Birkat Hamazon*.

The first is *Birkat Hazan*, which praises God for providing food for all. This prayer represents a public thanksgiving for Gods goodness to all humanity.

The second prayer is, *Birkat Haretz*, which includes two benedictions. The first benediction is *Nodeh Lecha*. This benediction gives thanks to God for all His past favors granted to our people. The second part of this benediction is *Val Hakol*, and this summarizes the preceding enumeration of blessings and concludes with a more formal form of benediction.

The third prayer is called *Boneh Yirushalim*, and it takes a totally different path. While the previous benedictions were expressions of gratitude for past favors, this prayer is for the future development of Zion.

Finally, the fourth prayer is *Hatov Vhamativ*. This prayer was added around 137 C.E. after the end of the *Bar Kochba* revolt upon the Roman authorities, allowing Jews to bury their dead.

So as you can see, there are some very good theological, historical and humanitarian reasons not to end a meal just with the check, but with a blessing. I hope that after understanding, on a deeper level, the *Birkat Hamazon*, our meals will taste better, for they will now be infused with the gratitude and knowledge of God.

31. THE AMIDAH -- STANDING BEFORE GOD

Yesterday, I wrote about the origins and makeup of *Birkat Hamazon*. Today, I would like to explore the origins of prayer and the *amidah*. Why do we pray and to whom are our prayers directed?

Do we look up towards the heavens and expect an immediate response? What happens if we don't receive that response? Do we give up on prayer or do we keep praying because that is what we *Jews do*?

In the *Talmud, Rabbi Yohanan* said: *Would that man would pray all day (Babylonian Talmud Berachot 21a)*. The implication is that man, when and as moved by the spirit, can commune with God and confront him.

During the Babylonian Exile (6th century B.C.E.) people were not able to sacrifice in the Temple, so they used prayer as a substitute for sacrifice.

The prophet Hosea summed this up when he wrote *The offerings of our lips instead of bulls (Hosea 14:2)*. People got together to pray three times a day, corresponding to the three daily sacrifices. The Jewish tradition concerning prayer, which evolved over time, prescribes *Shaharit,* the morning service, *Minhah,* the afternoon service and *Ma'ariv,* the evening service.

According to the sages of the *Talmud,* these services correspond to the three natural changes in the day: sunrise, approaching sunset, and night.

In the 5th century B.C.E, the *Men of the Great Assembly (Sanhedrin)* composed a basic prayer, covering just about everything you could want to pray about. This is the *Sh'moneh Esrei* which means *eighteen* and refers to the *eighteen blessings* originally contained within the prayer. It is also referred to as the *Amidah* (standing, because we stand while we recite it). This prayer is the cornerstone of every Jewish service.

The blessings of the *Sh'moneh Esrei* can be broken down into three groups: three blessings praising God, thirteen making requests (forgiveness, redemption, health, prosperity, rain in its season, ingathering of exiles, etc.), and three expressing gratitude and taking leave.

But wait! That makes *nineteen* and this prayer is called *eighteen.* How can we explain the difference between the name and the number of prayers?

The answer is that one of the thirteen requests (the one against heretics) was added around the second century C.E., in response to the growing threat of heresy. At that time, the prayer was already commonly known as the *Sh'moneh Esrei*, and the name stuck, even though there were now nineteen blessings.

Since the time of the Babylonian Exile, which I mentioned above, prayer has connected Jews wherever they may be and continues to bind us as a larger community today. Prayer has linked our religious and spiritual hearts, minds and souls for centuries and will, I hope, long into our future.

32. IS GOD'S LAUGHING AT US GOOD OR BAD?

During *Shabbat*, it is traditional to study Judaic texts and extrapolate meaning from them. However, whose extrapolated interpretations should we accept? How about the great theologians, *Rashi*, *Maimonides* and *Heschel*? What about our own interpretations, are they also legitimate? To answer this question, I looked toward *Pirkei Avot* for an answer, and there I found the following *Mishnah*.

Moses received the Torah at Sinai and handed it down to Joshua; Joshua to the elders; the elders to the prophets; and the prophets to the Men of the Great Assembly. They (the Men of the Great Assembly) said three things: Be deliberate in judgment; raise up many students; and make a fence for the Torah (PIrkei Avot 1:1).

From this passage, I find several teachings. First, *Torah* has been transmitted from one generation to the next. The purpose of this transmission allows each generation to study the texts and design its own additions to the literature. Moreover, the leaders of every generation may interpret and make the *Torah* relevant for their times.

TWO MINUTES OF TRADITIONS

The question that concerns me is, what did they mean in the phrase, *make a fence for the Torah?* The answer in my mind after pondering this question is that to make the *Torah* understandable and accessible for today's generation, we must ensure that our interpretations serve only to preserve the *Torah* and widen the belief and study of the *Torah*.

While we can widen the fence when we employ the disciplines of history and archeology to study *Torah*, we must always stay within the fence of reverence for, and loyalty to, the written text. We do not use modern science to destroy belief, but rather to make our beliefs stronger and more relevant to the current human condition. The following story from the *Talmud* concerning a dispute of Jewish law among our sages provides an example to this lesson.

If the halacha agrees with me, let it be proved from heaven! Whereupon a heavenly voice cried out: "Why do you dispute with Rabbi Eliezer seeing that in all matters of halacha (Jewish law) agrees with him?"

But Rabbi Joshua arose and exclaimed, "It is not in heaven!" What did he mean by this?

Said Rabbi Jeremiah; "That the Torah has already been given at Mount Sinai, therefore we pay no attention to a heavenly voice, because You have long since written in the Torah at Mount Sinai; After the majority must one not incline to pervert justice" (Exodus 23:2).

Rabbi Nathan met Elijah and asked him: "What did the Holy One, blessed be He, do at that hour?"

He replied: "He laughed, saying My sons have defeated me, My sons have defeated me" (Babylonian Talmud Baba Mezia 59a-b).

In other words, this story tells us that it is for us today to decide what Jewish law and learning is. Thus, any learning that we undertake to strengthen the fence around the *Torah* is a good thing.

I hope and pray that we all have time to study during this upcoming *Shabbat*, and I further want to thank you for learning with me this week.

33. MEMORIAL DAY

Today we mark Memorial Day here in the United States; a day to honor all those who died in military service and defense of our country. Memorial Day was born out of the Civil War and a want to honor all those who died in battle.

Memorial Day was officially declared on May 5th, 1868 by General John Logan. A national moment of remembrance resolution was passed in December of 2000, and it asks that all Americans in their own way voluntarily remember all those who have died in the service of our country at exactly 3:00 P.M. For more detailed information, go to your computer and check out the following URL.

www.usmemorialday.org

We are taught in the *Talmud* that, *He who saves one life, it is if they have saved the entire world (Babylonian Talmud Sanhedrin 37a)*, and this belief is appropriate today, as we remember all those who died while ensuring, through their service, that the world would be free and *saved* whenever and wherever needed.

As a former veteran, it has been my honor to officiate

at Memorial Day ceremonies in the past, as I will today, and I find it fitting for this morning to offer a prayer that I have adapted for these occasions;

Exalted, compassionate God, grant infinite rest, in Your sheltering Presence, among the holy and pure, to the souls of all our countrymen and heroes -- the men, women, and teenagers of the United States Military Forces who made the ultimate sacrifice in defense of these United States of America. Merciful One, we ask that our brothers and sisters, mothers and fathers, aunts and uncles, friends, acquaintances, strangers, and those who have nobody to remember them find perfect peace in Your eternal embrace. May their souls be bound up in the bond of life. May they rest in peace. And let us say; Amen.

Let us honor our heroes who have gone back to God, and always remember to thank those who have served and continue to serve, for their willingness to make the ultimate sacrifice on our behalf.

34. GOD'S DOMAIN

When we take out the *Torah* on *Shabbat* mornings, we sing the words *En Kamocha*.... which in English translates to, *None compare to You, O Lord, and nothing compares to Your creation. Your kingship is everlasting; Your dominion endures throughout all generations (Translation taken From Siddur Sim Shalom).*

This prayer, which is recited while the ark is being opened, holds multiple layers of meaning. If we were to look at the first part of the verse *(None compare to You....)*, we would recognize the fact that Judaism does acknowledge that other peoples and religions worship different gods.

However, at the same time, Judaism emphatically states that there are no other gods as unique and powerful as *Adonai*. This is what *Dr. Ben Sommer* calls the uniqueness of *Adonai's* monotheism. It is not the fact that there are no other gods in the world (Judaism has always acknowledged other peoples culture); rather, that there is none who is the ultimate God as *Adonai* is.

As a matter of fact, if we were to look at the history of

gods and creation, we would notice that *Adonai* is the only God who came into existence with creation, and in essence, He is the one who brought about creation. Furthermore, on closer inspection, we see that within other cultures, their dominant gods (who are portrayed as victors and vanquished over time – for example Chronus and Zeus), came into existence at least one or two generations after the creation of the world.

In terms of *Adonai*/God's *dominion and kingship being everlasting and throughout all generations*, this shows that *Adonai* is the only deity that is both within and outside the world for all times, both those times that we will experience and those which will go on without us.

The fact that this is sung in front of the open ark and in the presence of the *Torah*, reinforces the centrality of God in our communities and our lives. It is for this reason that we look towards the open ark when we praise God's name and not away from it, standing all the while, in honor of the creator of our universe.

35. HEBREW AS THE COMMON CORE LANGUAGE OF THE JEWISH PEOPLE

Yesterday, during Memorial Day, I was pondering the significance of English as the common core of our soldiers during training and in battle; specifically, how the language of commands and the common and shared principles that the military beset upon its soldiers crosses boundaries and ties together soldiers from all walks of life.

This led me to think about the significance of Hebrew for the Jewish people. If we were to look closely enough, we could conclude that the Hebrew language is ancient, sacred and one of the cornerstones of our heritage. In essence it binds Jews together no matter their place of origin or their religious practices. For we all pray in Hebrew, the *Torah* which we all read from is written in Hebrew and many of the commentaries that our modern day laws and customs are based upon were written in Hebrew.

Within the Hebrew language, there are words that are similar to each other, sharing the same root, which can teach us valuable lessons. Two such words are *echad* and *chedva*. The Hebrew word for oneness, *echad*, comes from the same root as the word for joy, *chedva*. We experience joy when we feel a sense of oneness and connectedness. An example of this can be found in the foundation of our people's monotheistic relationship with God. Abraham formulates a new relationship with God and is told *to go forth from your native land and from your father's house to the land that I will show you (Genesis 12:1)*.

Abraham is commanded to leave everything he knows behind and set forth to a place that God does not even name. God's words forces Abraham to change. Instead of fighting or doubting this upheaval, Abraham embraces it and prospers due to his new sense of joy and unity with God. Abraham finds *chedva (joy)* due to his new *echad (oneness)* with God.

It is my hope that through the remembrance of what unites us (God, *Torah*, History and more) that we can find joy in our own oneness with ourselves, our communities and God.

36. MY FAMILY --
THE LOURIES OR LURINIC KABBALAH?

Rabbi Isaac Luria (1534-72), was perhaps the most visionary and original of the theosophical *Kabbalists*. Luria offered novel insights into and interpretations of the classic *Kabbalistic* text, the *Zohar*, and his myth of creation, deconstruction and restoration became a dominant motif throughout later *Kabbalistic* and *Hasidic* thought.

Luria's theological and philosophical systems serve as an important foundation for today's *Kabbalistic* approach to contemporary theology, philosophy and psychology.

According to Luria, the creation of the world brought with it the extraction of something *(Yesh)* from the infinite *(Ein-Sof)*, when it arose within *Ein-Sof (the Infinite)*. To accomplish this Professor Mordecai Rottenberg of the Open University in Israel professes in his book *Jewish Psychology and Hasidism; The Psychology behind the Theology* that God performed an act of contraction *(Tzimzum)* and concealed Himself from a point, thereby forming a central, metaphysical void that had room for both God and humankind. It is in this void that the Primordial Man,

Adam Kadmon, and all the countless Worlds *(Olamot)* emerge.

Prof. Rabbi Adin Steinsaltz, the famed and world renowned Talmudist and head of the Aleph Society, stated that we live in *the worst of all possible worlds in which there is still hope,* yet, paradoxically it is the best of all possible worlds because it serves as the arena for redemption.

In this light, it is the task of individual men and women to extract those sparks *(netzotzim)* that are his or her fortune to encounter in life, and to raise and spiritualize them, so as to reconstitute and restore the harmony of God's original creation.

It is my hope and prayer that we can find the sparks of *Tikkun Olam, Gmilut Hasadim* and the Love of our Neighbor, for thus we will be extracting the sparks that can bring the warmth of *Torah* into humanity.

37. A PERSON'S NAME

Helping to select the name for another person is one of life's most exciting and challenging opportunities. Two nights ago (Tuesday), I was able to participate in the search of a name for a special person who will be converting to Judaism this morning. Ever since Adam and Eve, the human being has been granted the privilege and responsibility for choosing names for plants, animals, and yes, human beings (both adults and children).

Certain religious rituals require Hebrew names. Hebrew names are used for calling people to the *Torah*. Certain prayers, such as the memorial prayer *(El Maleh)* or the prayer for the sick *(misheberach)*, use the Hebrew name. Legal documents, such as the marriage document *(Ketubah)*, also use the Hebrew name.

There is a great deal of significance to one's name. The first of our matriarchs and patriarchs were childless when their names were Avram and Sarai. When they cried out in despair, what did God do? God changed Avram to Avraham. The *Talmud* and *Genesis Rabah* explain that Avram is a contraction of *av leAram*, father of Aram. Aram was Avraham's homeland. His original name indicates that he was a father to the people of Aram. He influenced this nation and showed the people the truth of monotheism.

The name Avraham is a contraction of the phrase *av hamon goyim,* father of a multitude of nations. The Talmud explains that this name means that Avraham will be the father of all the nations of the earth. Avraham's influence will extend beyond his homeland. All peoples will be affected by his teachings. The bestowal of the name Avraham implied that the Almighty will help Avraham communicate his message to all civilization.

In terms of Sarai, her name was changed to Sara, meaning a *princess of the world.* By changing their names, God changed their destiny. Their new names gave them a new fate in life. Shortly thereafter they had their child, Isaac. As we can see the name we are given at birth is very important, as is the name we earn during our lifetimes, for we are taught in *Pirkei Avot, Rabbi Shimon taught; There are three crowns; the crown of Torah, the crown of Priesthood, the crown of royalty, The crown of a good name is superior to them all (Pirkei Avot 4:17).*

So as the hours to today's conversion tick down, I am excited that not only will *Am Yisrael* gain another member of the covenant, but even more so that a good person and her good name will now officially be part of our community. *Mazal Tov* to us all!

38. BABY BOYS AND THE COVENANT OF CIRCUMCISION

This afternoon, the community and I will have the opportunity to share in a Jewish lifecycle event and that is a *Brit Milah (ritual circumcision)*. I first and foremost want to congratulate the family and wish them much health, happiness and *nachas* both today and in the future.

Of all the signs and symbols in the Jewish tradition, none is more widely known than circumcision. Circumcision for the Jewish people is the sign of the *b'rit*, the covenant between God and Israel, established first with Abraham and then renewed at Sinai, to be passed on through every generation.

Yes, circumcision is for us a sign that the Lord, who called to Abraham our father, calls yet to us of Abraham's seed, summoning us, *This is my covenant with them, says the Lord. My spirit is upon you and my words which I have put into your mouth shall not depart from your mouth, nor from your descendants mouth from now unto eternity (Isiah 59:21).*

We further read that, *God further said to Abraham: As for you, you shall keep My covenant, you and your offspring to come, throughout the ages. Such shall be to follow: every male among you shall be circumcised. You shall circumcise the flesh of your foreskin, and that shall be a sign of the covenant between Me and you. At the age of eight days, every male among you throughout the generations shall be circumcised...Thus shall My covenant be marked in your flesh as an everlasting pact (Genesis 17:9-13).*

Additionally in the *Talmud* we read that the rabbis said that every *mitzvah* for whom the children of Israel were willing to risk their lives remained with them *(Babylonian Talmud, Tractate Shabbat 139a)* and they gave circumcision as the example. As we can see, circumcision is at the center of Judaism's covenant with God and of central importance to both our past and our future.

It is with confidence in our continued flourishing as a people that I will attend the *brit* just a few hours before *Shabbat* and give thanks to God for the blessings that He has bestowed upon the baby, the family and all of *Am Yisrael*.

39. THE NEIGHBOR BEHIND THE FENCE

Only a few days ago, I was in the midst of a discussion concerning the upcoming holiday of *Shavuot*, which we will begin to celebrate at sundown on Tuesday evening. This conversation metamorphosed into a theological discussion of which laws lay at the heart of Judaism.

My answer was that while laws are at the heart of Judaism, for a large part, Jewish law is about love and brotherhood, and the relationship between man and his neighbors. Jewish law commands us to love both members of our communities as well as the *stranger among us (Leviticus 19:34),* to give aid to the poor and needy, and to do no wrong to anyone in speech or in business.

In fact acts of love and kindness are so much a part of Jewish law that the word *mitzvah (literally, commandment)* is commonly used to mean any good deed.

There are many examples of the principle *Love Thy Neighbor* in Judaism. The most well-known story has to do with Rabbi Hillel who lived around the time of Jesus (Hillel was in actuality a few decades older than Jesus, and there are many who believe that the theology of Jesus is based upon the principles of Hillel).

The famous story concerning Hillel tells us about a pagan who came to Hillel saying that he would convert to Judaism if Hillel could teach him the whole of the Torah in the time he could stand on one foot.

Hillel replied, *What is hateful to yourself, do not do to your fellow man. That is the whole Torah; the rest is just commentary. Go and study it (Babylonian Talmud Tractate Shabbat 31).*

In actuality we can find this principle in the *Book of Leviticus,* where we read *Love your fellow as yourself (Leviticus 19:18).*

This tradition of *loving thy fellow* continued to develop with one of the great if not the greatest Rabbi of all time, *Rabbi Akiba,* who lived around the second century of the Common Era. Rabbi Akiba stated that the principle of *loving thy fellow* is the essence of the *Torah*. My answer from my discussion of a few nights ago as to what lies at the foundation of Judaism is based upon this. I hope that during the upcoming week we can find a little more of Hillel's teachings within us.

40. REVELATION.
WHO, WHAT, WHEN AND WHERE

Shavuot, which is one of the three pilgrimage festivals, marks the receiving of the *Torah* by the Jewish people at Mount Sinai. Just a few days ago, while preparing for a class that I will be teaching on Tuesday night, I was asked *What are the Conservative movement's beliefs in relationship to revelation.*

There is no one particular answer, as the theologians of the movement hold differing views on this question. In general, Conservative Judaism, which occupies a more centralist position in American Judaism, offers a spectrum of positions regarding God's role in revelation. We will look at three of them. I hope that they offer some guidance on our movement's beliefs, and cause all of us to examine our own opinions on revelation.

Some Conservative theologians, such as the late *Abraham Joshua Heschel*, hold that God revealed *His Divine Will* at Sinai. Those revelations, however, were transcribed by human beings, which accounts for the wide variety of biblical traditions, and for the occasional contradiction of these traditions.

Other Conservative theologians, such as the late *Ben Zion Bokser,* hold that divinely inspired human beings wrote down the *Torah*. Thus the *Torah*, while written by man, is inspired solely by God.

Still others, such as the late *Seymour Siegel*, say *Torah* is the human record of the encounter between God and the Jewish people at Sinai. Since it was written by human beings, it contains some laws and ideas that we might reject as anachronistic.

These three are but a few of the opinions that our movement holds, but each one is central to how we can see the *Torah* as both heavenly and human. The nexus between the two is where we find ourselves in today's society, and is the meeting point where God and man converge.

I hope that the upcoming holiday of *Shavuot* will bring us to this point, and allow us the opportunity to delve into our own theologies on revelation, so that generations from now our commentaries will be added to the canon of Jewish opinions that have developed and been passed down until today. In the end we can say that Conservative Judaism sees *Torah* as an constantly evolving theology rooted in transcendent reality, and I hope that our theologies will also continue to evolve today and in the future.

41. KEEPING THE SABBATH HOLY

The Holiday of *Shavuot*, which we will be celebrating tonight, marks the day when the *Children of Israel* received the *Torah*. In the *Torah Parsha,* which we will read, we hear of the thrilling events, drama and special effects that surrounded Moses ascending and descending from Mount Sinai. Further into the *Parsha* we read the epitome of Judaism -- the *Ten Commandments.*

In the *Commandment* concerning keeping *the Sabbath Holy*, we read that we shall not work on the seventh day, for God created the world in six days and on the seventh He rested.

It is this statement which is found within the *Commandment of Keeping the Sabbath Holy* that has always bothered me, and especially bothers me on a day when we are taught about the receiving of the *Torah* and reminded of how the world was created!

You might be asking about now, what bothers me? My answer is the question, was the world really created in six days? As a modern member of society, I also accept the truths of science, and understand and even agree with many of the principles in the *Theory of Evolution.*

Thus it would seem that the two contradict one another. Either Science is correct and the *Torah* is wrong or the *Torah* is correct and Science is wrong. For it doesn't seem that there is any possibility that they can be congruent.

This controversy: of creationism vs. evolution is not a new one. In 1925 Scopes, was arrested for teaching the theory of evolution in Dayton, Tennessee. Scopes was vilified by *William Jennings Bryan* who claimed that the Bible was the true Teaching of creation.

In my own small way I would like to try and synthesize the two *(Torah and Evolution)* so we can truly be able to believe in the *Torah* while remaining true to our understanding and acceptance of modern science.

Let us look into the *Torah* first. The *Torah* tells us the story of creation in a gradual manner. First we read of light and darkness, than we read of sky and the water, and events eventually build up to the creation of animals and then culminates with Man.

In essence, we see gradual stages of creation. Not everything was created at once and Man (the highest form of creation) was only created at the very end of the process.

Now let us look at Evolution, which can be defined as the result of numerous changes in the molecular structure of all forms of life. This adaptation began with a mixture of atoms, and up until this point, culminates with man being the highest species of life form that we know of today.

Now since it seems possible, that these two very different realms of belief don't contradict each other in evolutionary development we are left with only one problem; that being, the problem of time.

The *Torah* says six days while science says millions of years. However this is easily solved as well, for we know that time in the *Torah* is not as we understand it today. A day is not necessarily 24 hours, and a year is not necessarily a year of 365 days. (An example is Noah who lived until 950 years old). If this is true, and a day solely represents a unit of time (unknown in length), then we can say that the development is similar, both in structure (man being last) and in time. Thus, I can celebrate both *Shavuot* and Science side by side and not one in contradiction to the other.

42. WHO'S GOT THE MOST GOLD?

The *Golden Rule* that society is built around, finds its foundation in the *Torah*. For there we read *Thou shalt love thy neighbor as thy love thyself (Leviticus 19:18).* The traditional commentary translation of the term *neighbor* does not refer to one's physical neighbor on either side of one's home, or across the street. Instead it widens the definition to mean *all good people in the world*, in essence all of humanity.

While, this may serve as the standard translation, there is a further explanation based upon *Psalm 23 where Adonai Roi is translated as The Lord is My Shepherd (Psalms 23:1).* From the word shepherd, *Rashi* in addition to the famous story of *Hillel, Shammai* and the proselyte in the *Babylonian Talmud Shabbat 31a,* defines neighbor (and thus the golden rule) in a completely different manner.

Rather, *Rashi* refers to neighbor as God, *What is hateful to you, do not do to your neighbor: Do not forsake your neighbor and your father's neighbor (Proverbs 27).* Here neighbor refers to the Holy One Blessed be He. Do not disobey His commandments for it is hateful unto you when a friend disobeys yours

TWO MINUTES OF TRADITIONS

(Rashi, Babylonian Talmud Shabbat 31a 'De-alekh Snie').

If we are to take *Rashi's* interpretation as correct, then God is our neighbor, which would imply that He is both in Heaven and on Earth, as well as being close to all those who recognize and accept His covenant.

Just yesterday we finished celebrating the holiday of *Shavuot (marks the Receiving of the Torah by the Children of Israel at Mount Sinai)* and reaffirming our covenant with God (our neighbor).

It is my hope and prayer that we will be able to integrate into our lives both the standard understanding of neighbor, as referring to humanity as a whole, as well as *Rashi's*, meaning God. For if we are successful in this, then we will have connected both society and God together in a way that will spread the *Golden Rule* for all. Let me wish each and every one of you *Shabbat Shalom* and a peaceful weekend.

43. THE LETTER OR THE SPIRIT OF THE LAW; WHICH IS MORE IMPORTANT?

One of the major theological questions that has permeated the Jewish community and its direction in terms of Jewish law, has always been; what is more important, the letter of the law or the spirit of the law?

In essence, do we follow the strict interpretations of *Halacha,* or attempt to implement the spirit of the laws as they were written?

To further blur the line between the two, the question of Jewish law can pertain to our interactions with human beings, as well as with inanimate objects and philosophical behaviors, just to mention a few of the possibilities. I will briefly bring one side of the argument, by quoting from the *Jerusalem Talmud*. There we read the story of the famous and virtuous *Shimon ben Shatah* who traded in cotton.

The story tells us that *One day, his students said to him: Master, allow us to buy you a donkey so that you will not have to labor so much! They went and bought him a donkey from a certain non-Jew, and found upon it a precious stone. He asked, "Does he know of it?'*

They replied, "No".

He told them, "Go and return it".

"But" they responded, "did not Rav Huna Bivi b. Gozlon say," quoting Rav: "It was stated in the presence of Rabbi, even according to the view that stealing from a heathen is forbidden, appropriating his lost property is permitted."

He responded, "What, do you think Shim ben Shatah is a barbarian? Shimon b. Shatah preferred hearing "Blessed be the God of the Jews, to all the riches of this world" (Jerusalem Talmud Bava Metzia 8b)

As we can see from this *midrash*, when it comes to human beings the spirit of the law and seeing the Godliness in each human being usually comes before the obscure law which may work in theory but not necessarily in practice.

While I am not advocating that the spirit of Jewish law is more important than the letter of the law in any and all manners, I am saying that when it comes to human beings, we must look at the individual and not solely the inanimate law that was written so many years ago. For as *Hillel* taught us *What is hateful to you, do not to your neighbor: that is the whole Torah (Babylonian Talmud Shabbat 31a).*

44. CHECKMARK JUDAISM

Yesterday, I wrote on the theological debate between the letter of the law and the spirit of the law in relationship to *halacha*. While this is without doubt an important question, it would seem to me that a person's intention would also have to be considered. Are we performing *Checkmark Judaism* or *Judaism with kavanah (intention/meaning)?*

My definition of *Checkmark Judaism* is; actions followed solely due to the fact they have been proscribed in the past, and continue to be followed (for any number of reasons) today. I believe that the *Talmud* offers us clues as to the importance of one's intentions when it comes to actions and the performance of *mitzvoth*.

In the *Babylonian Talmud* we read; *Said Rav Pappa to Abaye: "How is it that the former generations miracles were performed, and for us miracles are not performed? IT cannot be because of their superiority in study. We study more, have more to study, are more proficient... Yet when Rav Judah used to take off one shoe [at the beginning of a fast in time of drought], rain would fall; whereas we afflict ourselves and wail, and no notice is taken of us." Abaye said: "The former generations were willing to sacrifice their lives for the sanctification of God's name; we are not" (Babylonian Talmud Berachot 20a).*

In my mind this *midrash* is attempting to impart upon us this lesson -- that it is not our undertaking to add rules and restrictions onto past generations actions to look pious which is important, rather it is the intention of the individual when they fulfill a *mitzvah* or act for the sake of God that is central to how it is received in heaven.

In our example *Rav Pappa* didn't understand that it wasn't the aggregate of his actions that were counted, or his attempt to surpass *former generations* through the addition of *chumort (restrictions);* rather it was the devotional attitude of the former generation towards God which was central to their covenantal relationship being answered through miracles.

If we want to strive toward a closer relationship with God, I would suggest that it is not the fulfilling of *Checkmark Judaism* that is important, rather it is the intentions of our souls that lies at the core of our relationship with God.

45. DEVELOPMENT OF JEWISH LAW

Over the last two days, I have mentioned *Halacha,* without truly defining what it might be or where it comes from. During the upcoming day or two, I will, therefore, attempt to open our eyes to the development and source of Jewish law.

One of the first mentions of the need for an individual or group of individuals to interpret laws can be found in the *Book of Malachi. The priest's lips should keep knowledge, and they shall seek the law at his mouth.(Malachi 2:7)*

When a legal system has not yet been clearly codified, but is still, to a large extent, a mass of unorganized tradition, those who are the carriers of the tradition attain a special status. In the days of the temple the priest was the transmitter of the old tradition and, since there was no clear code, the only way for a person to know the law was to ask him. These personal inquiries inevitably took the form of correspondence. This was the beginning of the correspondence system, which gave birth to the *shallot (questions)* and *teshuvoth (answers),* around which the system of *halacha* was later built.

The need for a unified code of laws goes back as far into history as one can think. In a passage in the *Laws (722D-723B), Plato extols the value of accompanying codes of law and discrete laws with justificatory clauses. He compares the legislator to the physician; the free physician treating a free man explains and persuades, whereas the "servile physician treating a slave issues brusque injunctions."*

To prevent law from being *brusque injunctions*, one ought to add to each law a reason, a justification that states the rationale for the law. The law will then persuade and win the hearts of those whose obedience it seeks.

On this note, the term *halacha* is used in two different ways. It is generally used to signify the normative prescription or proscription that is the end result of the legal reasoning of a recognized *posek* or legalist. When used thus, the term ignores the process that led the *posek* to his conclusion, and its meaning is limited to the resultant norm.

The term *halacha*, however, is also used to signify the process by which legal conclusions are reached. In this sense the term refers to all of the factors that must or that might be considered by a *posek* before rendering his *pesak (decision)*. When all of these factors are expounded together with the resultant norm, it rarely appears simple, clear, or definitive. It is, rather, complex, ambiguous and replete with grounds for disagreement among *posekim*. Tomorrow, we will delve into the principles that guide this complex legal system among the varying opinions of *posekim (decision makers)*.

46. HALACHA

Continuing our discussion of *Halacha* from yesterday, we can learn that the term *halacha*, is used to signify the process by which legal conclusions are reached. In this sense the term refers to all of the factors that must or that might be considered by a *posek (determiner of Jewish Law)* before rendering his *pesak (decision)*.

As a legal process, *halacha* is governed by systemic principles; that is, principles that govern the way in which the process works, as opposed to those that govern determination of the law in any given case within the system. The latter are legal principles. Certain legal principles are also systemic principles, but many systemic principles are not legal in nature at all.

Systemic principles fall into two categories; explicit and implicit. Explicit principles are those that have been stated in the legal literature, while implicit principles are those that can be deduced from the myriad sources available to the *posek*, even though they have not been explicitly stated. In essence when considering a question of *halacha* both legal precedent and modern cultural norms are taken into consideration, and often intertwined in the final conclusion.

The final and most important question that we need to ask is, who may interpret Jewish law? The answer to this can be found in the *Talmud*, where we read; *"If the halacha agrees with me, let it be proved from heaven." Whereupon a heavenly voice cried out: "Why do you dispute with R. Eliezer seeing that in all matters of halacha agrees with him?" But R. Joshua arose and exclaimed; "it is not in heaven!" What did he mean by this Said R. Jeremiah; "That the Torah has already been given at Mount Sinai, therefore we pay no attention to a heavenly voice, because You have long since written in the Torah at Mount Sinai; After the majority must one incline" (Exodus 23:2) R. Nathan met Elijah and asked him: "What did the Holy One, blessed be He, do at that hour" He replied: "He laughed, saying My sons have defeated me, my sons have defeated me." (Babylonian Talmud Baba Mezia 59a-b)*

The message of this story is quite clear. God gave us the *Torah* at Mount Sinai. God then relinquished his right to interpret and change it. This responsibility he gave to the sages of each generation. Thus Jewish law is constantly changing and evolving, and I, for one, think this is part of the reason that it has remained alive and vibrant for thousands of years.

I hope the last two days writings on *halacha* (which if studied in depth could and has been written in multivolume studies) has given you a bit more clarification as to how rabbinic Judaism has developed over the last 2000 years.

47. I'M ON FIRE: IS THE ETERNAL LIGHT ONLY IN THE TEMPLE?

We often ask, how can we as a people survive? I believe that part of the answer can be found in one of the central ritual pieces found within a sanctuary -- the *Eternal Light* that hangs above the ark. We find, in the book of *Leviticus*, the mention of a perpetual fire, for there it is written, *A perpetual fire shall be kept burning on the altar, not to go out (Leviticus 6:6).*

The priests were commanded to keep the flames of the altar continually burning by adding wood every day, stoking the fire and keeping watch. This dedication was impressive, and should serve as an example about dedication in our own lives. The question that needs to be asked is, what did this perpetual flame symbolize and how is it relevant today? I would like to put forward three possibilities, each offering us a chance for personal relevance.

My late rabbinical school teacher, Prof. Zeev Falk Z"L, offered up that perpetual fire *expresses the presence of God's indwelling.* For it was not enough to just offer sacrifices whose aim was to bring the Israelites closer to God's presence, rather there needed to be a visual symbol in their midst at all times. Further, fire, has both divine and human qualities *(God created, and man must care for the flames and warmth within the world)*. So too the *Torah*, God gave, and man must tend after it.

In *Proverbs,* we read the words *guard the commandments of your fathers and do not abandon the Torah of your mothers; tie them to your heart always. (Proverbs 6:21).* The teaching here is that *Torah* binds us together.

Furthermore, after the destruction of the second temple Israelites could no longer make physical offerings, so they needed other ways to keep their spiritual flame burning. Daily prayers became the way to keep that flame burning, as important as sacrifices.

Rabbi David Lazar once wrote that innovation in prayer is another way to keep our perpetual lights burning. Finally we learn from the *Baal Shem Tov that a Jew should serve God with ardor.* In essence he was telling us to have the eternal sparks of God within us at all times.

Here we have the three models/interpretations as to what the eternal light is and how it is relevant today. Now it is up to us to find a that we feel is appropriate to keep our individual and communal perpetual fire burning. For this is how we shall ensure our future. *Shabbat Shalom,* and may the fire of God light up our own perpetual lights.

48. FATHER'S DAY

On a day like today (i.e. Father's Day), I am left to ponder the founding father of monotheism. Of course I am speaking of *Avraham (Abraham)* our first patriarch. However, *Avraham* was not always known by this name. The first time we meet him in the *Torah*, his name is *Avram*.

Hebraically, the letter *Hey* that is missing between *Avram* and *Avraham's* names, represents in traditional Judaism an abbreviation for God's name. The transformation of *Avram's* name can be found in the *Book of Genesis in Parshat Lech-Lecha* where we read the following verse; *You shall no longer be called "Avram," but rather "Avraham," because I have made you a father of many nations (Genesis 17:5).*

The question that remains for us is, why was *Avraham* chosen by God? One of the answers that is particularly relevant for us today can be found in the *Book of Nehemiah*, where we read *You are Adonai, the God who chose Avram and brought him out of Ur of the Chaldees: You named him Avraham, and found in his heart a faithful servant (Nehemiah 9:7-8).*

Here we see that our first father, *Avraham*, was chosen by God for his faithful heart and his fidelity to the morals and teachings that monotheism brought with it. A further commentary on *Avraham's* name can be found in the numerical value of his name *(Gematriah)*, which equals 248. This number is important for we are taught in the *Talmud* that 248 is not only the numerical number of *Avraham's* name, but also the number of bones in a human being *(Babylonian Talmud Nedarim 32a)*.

From this we can conclude that *Avraham* loved God with his entire being, and thus was worthy of becoming the first patriarch (father) of monotheistic humanity. As fathers and children ourselves we can learn from our first patriarch, that the essence of our souls should be based in morality and fidelity; morality within the world around us, and fidelity to our families.

It is my hope and prayer that on this *Father's Day*, we will find in the example of *Avraham* from *Parshat Lech-Lecha* and the commentaries that I mentioned, an inspiration to become better parents and children within the world around us. Let me take this opportunity to wish all the fathers in our society a happy and healthy Father's Day.

49. THE GREEN HEAD OF JEALOUSY

In this week's *parsha, Korach*, we learn about the dangers of jealousy. Jealousy as defined by the Webster's dictionary is; *an unhappy or angry feeling of wanting to have what someone else has (noun as defined in Webster.com).*

When we examine the actions of *Korach*, we can find that he was jealous of Moses, due to the fact that he believed that Moses had put himself above the congregation as seen in the *Book of Numbers*. If we were to translate *Korach's* actual comments, *Why have you placed yourselves above the Congregation of God (Numbers 16:3)*, we would find that *Korach* is motivated by jealousy.

Why? Because even though he is a Levite, he isn't on the same level as Moses in terms of respect from the Israelites or covenantal closeness to God. It is this jealousy that causes *Korach* to challenge Moses, and thus God Himself. What is the outcome of this jealousy? The death of *Korach* and all of his followers! What *Korach* did not understand, was the fact that each member within the *Children of Israel* was valued in his/her own way by God. When one didn't understand the importance of the whole, then that individual put himself outside the community. With this sort of behavior, *Korach* lost everything.

Human beings often look at what others have and want the same for themselves. In other words, we become jealous. The goal that we should strive toward is appreciating who we are and what we are blessed with, for richness doesn't come with status. This is something that *Korach* refused to understand.

Richness comes from being happy with one's own lot in life, just as *Pirkei Avot* taught us over 1500 years ago with the words, *Who is wealthy? He who is happy with his lot (Ethics of the Fathers 4:1)*, and thus our lesson for today is to follow the teachings of our sages and not the actions of *Korach*. For in this we will find not only reward in this world within our communities, but additionally reward within our souls for becoming closer to God.

50. UNDERSTANDING GOD

The actions and eventual death of *Korach* are known to us all, through the retelling of his story in this week's *parsha*. Yesterday we spoke about the jealousy that *Korach* held in his heart towards Moses, which, in my mind, was compounded due to his lack of understanding the true meaning and omnipotence of God.

On the other hand, this same lack of understanding can't be said about his sons, and this we know through the examination of a number of Psalms that are attributed to them *(i.e. Psalms 47-49)*. Psalm 47 begins with the following formula, *To the chief Musician: A Psalm for the sons of Korach (Psalm 47:1)*, and then continues on with a description of God's power. It is toward the end of the *Psalm*, where the true recognition of God's unique attributes is mentioned by *Korach's* sons.

For there we read; *Sing praises to God, sing praises: sing praises to our King, sing praises. For God is the king of all the earth: sing a Maskil psalm. God reigns over the nations: God sits upon the throne of his holiness. The nobles of the peoples are gathered together, the people of the God of Avraham: for the shields of the earth belong to God; he is greatly exalted (Psalm 47; Koren Publishers Jerusalem Bible-English Text revised and edited by Harold Fisch).*

From this verse we can conclude that the sons of *Korach* based upon their first-hand knowledge and experiences during their father's revolt, understood that no human being or group of human beings could ever challenge God for control over the earth. Thus the proper way to behave was by praising God's power.

The lesson for our generation, in my mind, is to always remember that the ultimate power resides with God and not with man. Accepting this will allow us to not only enjoy the Psalms, but also to understand them.

51. PSALM 30 AND OUR EMOTIONS

Every day in the morning blessings directly preceding the *Mourners Kaddish* and *P'sukei D'Zimra (Verses of Songs)*, *Psalm 30* is chanted. This *Psalm*, which is credited to David and dedicated to the Temple, is and of itself, centered on the theme of God's deliverance of the individual in times of distress.

The words of redemption and the divine grace of God towards the individual author can be found in numerous verses, such as *Adonai, I cried out and You healed me. You saved me from the pit of death....You transformed my mourning into dancing, my sackcloth into robes of joy -- that I might sing Your praise unceasingly, that I might thank You, Adonai my God, forever (Psalm 30 vs. 3-4, 12-13).*

Looking closely at these verses, we can understand a multitude of emotions that the author was feeling at the time he spoke them. In my mind, it makes sense that he had just gone through an extreme period of danger (physical, emotional or spiritual – any one of these or any combination of them is fitting), and has now been saved.

Having come through to the other side of this danger,

the writer is trying to relay his conclusion of that experience to the reader. Those conclusions being, that in times of trouble and travail, only the power of God in combination with man's belief could have pulled him through the life changing event that he just experienced.

Moreover, we could conclude that the author's belief had been strengthened for having survived such an ordeal, for had it already been strong, there would have been no need to write such a *Psalm of deliverance*. The final conclusion that I will mention today that stems from this *Psalm* is personal and relates to each and every one of us.

This being that we too go through hard times during our lives, and with the power of belief we can also survive the trials and tribulations that we face. For in difficult times, just as the famous poem *Footsteps in the Sand* teaches us, it is not that we are walking alone through life. Rather during the hard times, it is God who is carrying us. This affords us the opportunity to move forward, even when all we want to do is to lie down, curl up and hide from the world.

52. BUBEE, GRANDMA, MOM AND THE NEXT GENERATIONS: CONNECTION OR DISCONNECT?

I was asked the other day in my *For Women Only* class, why is today's generation distancing themselves from the *Judaism of our parents, grandparents and great grandparent's generations?*

While striving for an answer to this existential question and identity crisis that we are facing, I remembered that towards the end of the *Book of Exodus*, we read about the *Mishkan (Tabernacle)* that was built by the *Children of Israel* during their travels and travails in the desert.

It would be logical to think that the *Mishkan* itself, once built, would be the final religious institutional development for the *Children of Israel* while they were in the desert. Nonetheless, while we do see that once built, the *Mishkan* became the center of religious worship, as led by the *Cohanim,* as well as the place for God's essence to reside, this was not the end of the story. For we are witnesses to the fact that the *Children of Israel* had to remain dynamic and ever evolving in order to reach the Land of Israel.

Similarly, with the foundation of the State of Israel and

the growth of World and American Jewry, one might think that we, too, have completed our *Mishkan* and it is time to rest on our past successes. However, we, like the *Children of Israel* in the desert, need to remain dynamic and move forward, while at the same time continuing to develop. The question being, how do we accomplish this?

In my opinion, an answer to this question can be found in the *Babylonian Talmud*. In *Tractate Baba Batra*, we read that *one learns piety through pursuing it. (Babylonian Talmud Baba Batra 10a)*. In essence the *Talmud* is trying to teach us that we should act and not only learn; lead and not only follow; and give without expectation of receiving. In other words our actions should mimic those of the *Children of Israel* who mouthed at the foot of Mount Sinai, *Naseh V'nishma* which can be translated as *everything the Lord has spoken we will do (Exodus 24:8)*.

Thus we are prompted to act in a way which enhances holiness in our lives and in the larger community. This we can do with the enhancement of spirituality, religiosity, *tikkun olam (repairing the world)*, observance of *mitzvoth* and *Halacha* and much more. For Judaism, over the past millennia, has laid out a path of development and covenantal life from which we can learn and emulate.

If we are able to act in such a manner, then we will truly be fulfilling the *mitzvah* of building holy communities within *Am Yisrael*. This is the answer that we all must answer, and the challenge that lies in front of us if we want to engage future generations in the rich traditions of Judaism and all that it has to offer.

TWO MINUTES OF TRADITIONS

53. SCHOOLS OVER? REALLY?

I was driving my daughter to PSAT camp the other day, and saw the school warning lights blinking. These lights were telling us to drive slowly as students are in the area. At the same time I saw the lights blinking, I saw a sign outside the school that said, and I paraphrase, *Schools Over: Enjoy your summer and be safe.*

The words *Schools Over* brings out in me a personal curiosity as to what the Jewish sources have to say about the essence of one half of the two words we have just mentioned. That being the word *school,* or a *Bet Midrash (house of study)* as it is known in Hebrew.

One of the earliest references to a *Bet Midrash* can be found on a *Midrash* which deals with the biblical brothers Jacob and Esau. *Rabbi Phinehas said in Rabbi Levi's name: They were like a myrtle and a wild rose-bush growing side by side; when they attained to maturity, one yielded its fragrance and the other its thorns. So for thirteen years both went to school and came home from school. After this age, one went to the house of study and the other to idolatrous shrines (Genesis Rabba 63:10).*

What does this text teach us? On the surface it

teaches us that both Jacob and Esau studied until the age of 13, and afterwards only one continued in the study of *Torah* while the other left his studies and came under the influence of idolatry. However underneath this simple explanation, the text is trying to teach us something of much greater import. That formal education alone is not enough. One must also have a love of learning and a willingness to learn to be able to reap the full benefits that education has to offer.

This source also teaches us that learning must never stop, *school is never over.* For if we stop learning as individuals we might get caught up in non-positive activities just like Esau got caught up with idolatry.

The *Bet Midrash's* importance became even more evident during the period in which the *Talmud* was written (between 200-500 C.E.). There we read that *A scholar should not reside in a city where the following ten things are not found: A court of justice that imposes flagellation and decrees penalties; a charity fund collected by two and distributed by three; a Synagogue; public baths; a convenience; a circumciser; a surgeon, a notary; a slaughterer and a school-master (Sanhedrin 17b).*

This Talmudic passage sets up a guideline for a proper city. The city itself must contain institutions that will tend to the spiritual, hygienic, health, religious and educational needs of all who live there. The fact that the schoolmaster is in this list shows in my mind the importance and added emphasis that education must be given in any and all communities.

This *Shabbat* makes it possible for us to take a little more time to try and educate ourselves to the weekly *parsha* and the *Shabbat* prayers, so that we will become like, and be remembered like our patriarch; Jacob, a man of intellect who was touched by, and spoke with, God.

54. STRESS IN OUR LIVES

Many of us lead hectic and stressful lives. To alleviate some of the stress of everyday life, we try to find paths that calm our bodies and our souls. Some of us work out at a gym. Others alleviate their stress through any number of hobbies. The most important thing is that we each find something that we love to participate in.

One of the ways that I have found comfort on many occasions in the past is through singing *zmirot (songs)* and *nigunim (melodies)*. One of my favorite songs is one of the most poetic and beautiful love songs that I have ever encountered. It is so beautiful that many brides walk down to their *chuppah (wedding canopy)* with this song in the background. The song is called *Erev Shel Shoshanim (Night of Roses)*. Written by Moshe Dor, it reads:

An evening of roses. Let us go out to the orchard. Myrrh, spices and frankincense shall be as a threshold for your feet.

The night comes upon us slowly and a breeze of roses is blowing.

Let me whisper a song to you quietly, a song of love.

TWO MINUTES OF TRADITIONS

It is dawn, a dove is cooing, Your hair is filled with dew.

Your lips are like a rose to the morning,

I'll pick it for myself.

To me this song talks about love, between a man and a woman, a boyfriend and girlfriend, a husband and wife, or two committed partners. This song evokes love not only for the outer beauty of a partner, but also for that person's inner beauty. This song touches me because it sings about the beauty and wonders of nature.

Those wonders can be found in the beauty of the roses, the spices, the breeze of the nights and the beauty of a dove. The song speaks to the beauty both of human beings and the natural world. Finally I find the description of the twilight hours to be magnificent.

I often ask myself why am I more attracted to this song than to others? The answer is; because the relationship in this song is more than a bond between two people; it is also a connection between God and us.

As I mentioned earlier, this is a song of brides, and this morning, we at *Ahavath Sholom* will have the opportunity to sing *(actually the Cantor will have the opportunity to sing as the rest of us enjoy)* this love song as a bride (Eszter Vandaveer) walks down towards the *Chuppah.* On behalf of our entire congregation, we wish her and Glenn, *Mazal Tov* and may they always stand under the *Chuppah of Happiness*.

For a rendering of this endearing love song, go to your computer and follow this link. It is well worth your time.

http://www.youtube.com/watch?v=umJ0a8x0Oxw

55. CHOSEN? CHOSEN BY WHOM AND WHAT DOES THIS MEAN?

I have heard throughout my life the statement, *Since you are the chosen people, you must think that you are better than others.* (an often used anti-Semitic argument). As a matter of fact a message with the same intention was left anonymously on my phone a few weeks ago. While I was not able to answer such a message, I do think that I can offer a response for all of us to use.

What we need to respond is that the opposite is actually true, for contrary to popular belief Judaism not only tells us to *love thy fellow,* but also teaches us that we are not better than any other nation. Although we refer to ourselves as God's chosen people, we do not believe that God chose us because of any inherent superiority.

According to the *Talmud (Avodah Zarah 2b)*, God offered the *Torah* to all the nations of the earth. The *Children of Israel* were the only ones who accepted it. The story goes on to say that the *Children of Israel* were offered the *Torah* last, and accepted it only because God held a mountain over their heads *(Exodus 19:17)*.

Another traditional story suggests that God chose the *Children of Israel* because they were the lowliest of nations, and their success would be attributed to God's might rather than their own ability. Clearly, these are not the ideas of a people who think they are better than other nations.

In addition, according to traditional Judaism, God gave *Noah* and his family seven commandments to observe when he saved them from the flood. These seven commandments, referred to as the *Noahic of Noahide* commandments, are inferred from *Genesis Ch. 9*, and are as follows:

1. To establish courts of justice
2. Not to commit blasphemy
3. Not to commit idolatry
4. Not to commit incest and adultery
5. Not to commit bloodshed
6. Not to commit robbery
7. Not to eat flesh cut from a living animal.

These commandments are fairly simple and straightforward, and most of them are recognized by most of the world as sound moral principles. Tradition teaches us that these seven laws should be the foundation for all nations throughout the world.

It is further taught that any non-Jew who follows these laws has a place in the world to come. Here once again we see that a man is judged on his merits and the way he lives and not by the religion he was born into or chooses to associate himself with.

Finally I believe that Judaism's respect for all human life, Jewish or not, can be found in a story about the great late Rabbi and Talmudist who lived in last century, *Rabbi Prof. Saul Lieberman.*

It is told that one day on Shabbat, Prof. Lieberman was walking with a good friend of his who happened to be non-Jewish. During their walk together they both happened to walk under the scaffold of a building that was being repaired. Prof. Lieberman's friend turned to him and stated that *according to strict Jewish law on the Sabbath if the scaffold fell on a fellow Jew, then Prof. Lieberman could transgress any Shabbat laws to save him. However, his friend went on to say, If the same scaffold fell on him, who was non-Jewish, then Prof. Lieberman would not be able, according to strict Jewish law, to save him.*

At this point his friend asked Prof. Lieberman what he would do if this actually happened, and the scaffold was to fall upon him (the non-Jew). Prof. Lieberman answered him, saying, *I would first save your life and then find a reason whereby Judaism would allow this.*

Lieberman went on to say that this would not be hard for we are commanded as we have seen *to love thy neighbor as one loves thyself.*

I think that this story sums up Judaism's respect for all human life, not just our own, and is the answer to anyone who claims that we feel superior to all others.

56. HOW DO WE PRAY?

When students from TCU (Texas Christian University) call me for an interview so that they can write a term paper on Judaism, or when individuals who are contemplating converting call, they all ask the same question; *How do you pray in your religion and synagogue?*

My answer usually centers on a famous story about personal prayer that grew out of *Chasidism*, and its founder, known as the *Ba'al Shem Tov (1700-1762).*

The *Ba'al Shem Tov* taught that, while learning and knowledge were important in the service of God, more than anything else, God desired the most faithful devotion of one's heart. The following *Midrash* demonstrates the powerful feeling that personal prayer can bring about;

A villager who went to town every year on the High Holy Days to pray in the synagogue of the Ba'al Shem Tov, had a son who was so simple that he could not even learn the Hebrew alphabet, much less a single prayer. And because the boy knew nothing, his father never brought him to town for the holidays. Yet, when the boy reached the age of thirteen and became responsible for his actions, his father decided to take him to the synagogue on Yom HaKippurim, lest he stay at home and, in his ignorance, eat on the holy fast day.

And so they set out together - and the boy, who had a little flute on which he used to play to his sheep, unbeknownst to his father, put the flute into his pocket. In the middle of the service, the boy, touched by the power of the prayers, suddenly said, "Father, I want to play my flute!" The horrified father scolded his son and told him to behave himself. A while later, though, the boy said again, "Father, please let me play my flute!" Again his father scolded him, warning him not to dare; yet soon the boy said a third time, "Father, I don't care what you say, I must play my flute!"

"Where is it?" asked the father seeing that the boy was uncontrollable. The boy pointed to the pocket of his jacket, and his father seized it and gripped it firmly so that the boy could not take out his little flute. And so the hours passed with the man holding onto his son's pocket.

The sun by now was low in the sky, the Gates of Heaven began to close, and it was time for the final prayer of the day (Ne'ilah). Halfway through the closing prayer, the boy wrenched the flute free from his pocket and his father's hands, put it to his mouth, and let out a loud blast that startled the entire congregation.

As soon as the Ba'al Shem Tov heard it, he hurried through the rest of the service, as he had never done before. Afterward, when asked by his followers, he told them "when this little boy played his flute, all your prayers soared heavenward at once and there was nothing left for me to do but finish up."

The lesson that this *Midrash* wants to teach us, in my mind, is that personal prayer and praying in any manner that moves you is what God wants from us, and this is the answer to anyone who wants to know how we pray in Judaism and here at *Congregation Ahavath Sholom*.

57. PSALM FOR THE DAY AHEAD

The Book of Psalms is a very moving and intellectually deep understanding of the human psyche and soul as seen through the connection to the self, community and God. The themes within the psalms differ in many ways. There are some that speak about God's omnipotence, His love of humanity and the *Children of Israel*, deliverance in times of distress, hope, glory and much more.

Furthermore there are psalms which are recited daily, for example *(Psalm for the Day)* and some that are said individually at different times and under different circumstances.

Immediately upon wrapping ourselves in the *Tallit*, which is to remind us of all of God's *mitzvoth*, and saying the blessing in the morning, a number of verses are read from *psalm 36*. Those verses read;

How precious is Your constant love, O God. Mortals take shelter under Your wings.

They feast on the abundance of Your house; You give them drink from Your stream of delights.

With You is the fountain of life; in Your light we are

bathed in light. Maintain Your constant love for those who acknowledge You, and Your beneficence for those who are honorable (Psalm 36: 8-11).

This *Psalm* is making two theological statements that are in essence interconnected. The first deals with God's constant love and his generosity and protection of the individual, while the second states that this love is restricted to only the honorable.

These two statements come together to teach us the path that we should follow in life and the reward that is bestowed upon us for living the path of honor. The recitation of these verses are, in actuality, a daily reminder as to how we should live our life and why we should be thankful to God. Once this has been realized, we can continue on into the opening blessings and the rest of the morning service.

58. LEADERS WHO HAVE LET US DOWN

Headline: from walla.co.il; Former Israeli Presidential Candidate and Defense Minister, Binyamin Ben-Eliezer, is under suspicion of having accepted bribes and using his influence to help a businessman develop his business relationships in Egypt. Police have announced that his bank accounts are like a Pandora box. While of course Ben Eliezer is presumed innocent until proven guilty, I am still personally both disheartened and tired of the wrongdoing that our *rulers* have done.

The *Torah* teaches what the leader should do when the offense is made public: *In case it is a chieftain who incurs guilt by doing unwittingly any of the things which by the commandment of the Lord his God ought not to be done, and he realizes his guilt – or the sin of which he is guilty is brought to his knowledge – he shall bring as his offering a male goat without blemish. (Leviticus 4:22-23)*

I am afraid that some of our former *chieftains* both in America and Israel never learned these verses. We've had President Nixon and the Watergate scandal that led to his resignation, while in Israel, former President, Moshe Katzav is now sitting in jail for sexual offences perpetrated against a number of young women who served under him, and former Prime Minister, Ehud Olmert was recently convicted of taking $140,000 in bribes and has been sentenced to six years in prison.

Currently Olmert is appealing his sentence. Nonetheless, not one of these politicians ever made a formal acknowledgment of his wrongdoing.

The behavior of these leaders is not acceptable today and has never been acceptable among the *Children of Israel*. For when a ruler has sinned even unknowingly, he must offer a sacrifice and make atonement. We know this because in the *Babylonian Talmud* we read: *Rabbi Johanan ben Zakkai said: Happy is the generation whose ruler brings a sacrifice for a sin he has committed unwillingly. If its ruler brings a sacrifice, is there any need to say what one of the common people would do: and if he brings a sacrifice for a sin he has committed unwillingly, is there any need to say what he would do in case of a sin committed willfully? (Babylonian Talmud Masechet Horayoth 10b).*

In this passage Rabbi Johanan ben Zakkai is praising a generation due to the actions of its rulers. *Happy is the generation*: Why is the generation happy, one could ask? Is it because the *ruler* acts in the same manner that he demands from his people? Is it because both the *ruler* and his people are equal in God's eyes? Is it possibly because the *ruler* in this case sets a personal example for his people? Maybe the generation would be *happy* because they would now have a *ruler* who would be to his people a moral compass upon which they could direct their own lives.

In the end, I think all three of these reasons were true; for a ruler with a high level of morality is one that always makes his people strive to be better themselves. I wish it were this sort of lesson that I was teaching about, instead of having to react to another fallen politician who has let down his family, constituents and trust in government.

59. V'SHAMRU

During *Friday Night Kabbalat HaShabbat* services, the beautiful and meaningful prayer, *V'shamru* is sung. The prayer itself has been recited for approximately 1400 years, beginning in the Gaonic Period (600-1000 C.E.). The Gaonic Period was the period of the two great Babylonian Academies (Sura and Pumbedita), and the geonim were the spiritual leaders and Presidents of the academies at that time.

The prayer itself is translated in the following manner *And the children of Israel shall keep the Sabbath and eternal covenant for their generations. Between Me and the Children of Israel it is a sign forever that in six days Hashem [God] made heaven and earth, and on the seventh day He rested and was refreshed (Translation from The Complete ArtScroll Siddur by Rabbi Nosson Scherman-Mesorah Publications pg. 337).*

Thematically we see that the prayer is centered around *B'nai Israel (Children of Israel)* and the importance of their covenantal relationship developed with God through the *keeping and observing (Fourth Commandment as seen in words Shamor V'Zachor from L'cha Dodi) of Shabbat.* Moreover we know from the teachings of Rabbi Yechiel Michel Epstein (1829-1908), compiler and writer of *Aruch HaShulchan*, that if one observes Shabbat, Shabbat will protect him *(Aruch Hashulchan, O.H. 267:7).*

As we can see the theological dimension of *V'shamru* has to do with the relationship between *Man and God*, as well as the *guarding of Shabbat* being a two way assurance. On the one hand, if we as human beings are to *guard the Shabbat* our relationship with God will be strengthened, and on the other hand, *Shabbat* is our guardian as well.

I hope that we will all have the opportunity to recite these words this evening, and I enclose a clip to a beautiful version of the prayer for your enjoyment. Shabbat Shalom

http://www.youtube.com/watch?v=u5dO1m4HMCU

60. SHARK TANK AND BEING RICH

Mark Cuban, Kevin O'Leary, Daymond John, Robert Herjavec and Lori Greiner are the judges on a CNBC show called Shark Tank. The premise of the show is that budding inventors and entrepreneurs come before the panel of judges (sharks) to pitch their idea/product and, in essence, themselves, in the hopes, that one of the panel of *sharks* will invest in their company in return for equity in that company.

During the introduction to the show, the panel is introduced, including a short bio of how much each one is worth, and how each one made his/her money is mentioned.

This show while entertaining, does not speak about true wealth as Judaism sees it. If we were to take the word *Ashir (Rich)* in Hebrew, we would notice that it is composed of four letters (*Ayin, Shin, Yud* and *Reish*). If we were further to take each letter individually, we could see, if we looked closely enough, that each letter offers us a clue as to who is truly rich. The first letter, *Ayin* introduces the word *Aiyniyem (Eyes)*, the second letter *Shin* might stand for *Shyinayim (Teeth),* the third letter *Yud* represents *Yadayim (Hands)* while the last letter *Reish* leaves us with *Reglayim (Legs).* If we were to put all of these letters together, *Ashir* equates to; Eyes, Teeth, Hands and Legs.

In essence, Judaism is trying to teach us, that the truly wealthy person is one who has his health. I hope that as we mark the new month of *Tammuz* this morning, we will realize that the truly wealthy are not the *sharks* sitting as judges on the show, rather those who wake up in the morning and live a life of health. Let me wish everyone a week filled with health and happiness.

PART II

RABBINIC REFLECTIONS

THE THEME OF REDEMPTION

May God grant all of us a good and healthy New Year and may we all be inscribed in the book of life. As I write this article the High Holy Days are right around the corner. It seems that just yesterday the summer started but alas its waning days are upon us. This causes me to think of the past year and what I hope and pray for during the upcoming year. In the quiet moments of solitude that I find for reflection I often look back towards a prayer that can be found during the *Zikhronot (God remembers)* part of our service that is recited during *Musaf* (the service after the returning of the *Torahs* to the Ark) of Rosh Hashanah.

The prayer is as follows: *A man cannot find redemption until he sees the flaws in his soul, and tries to efface them. Nor can a people be redeemed until it sees the flaws in its soul and tries to efface them. But whether it be a man or a people, whoever shuts out the realization of his flaws is shutting out redemption. We can be redeemed only to the extent to which we see ourselves.*

The question, which arose in me when I first read this prayer years ago, was; *I thought that the Messiah was going to redeem us?*

For after all, during our daily prayers in the *Amidah* we ask that God should; *Bring to flower the shoot of Your servant David. Hasten the advent of the Messianic redemption; Each and every day we hope for Your deliverance. Praised are You, O Lord, who assures our deliverance.*

While this prayer asks for the *Messiah* to come; in my view it does not detract from the prayer we say on *Rosh Hashanah,* rather it enhances it. For the *Messiah* that we all hope will come one day and bring peace to the world can only arrive once each and every one of us as individuals bring peace into our own souls.

How do we do this? In my mind I have noticed that the prayer during *Rosh Hashanah* talks about realizing our flaws. While we all know that Jewish Mothers around the world often repeat the same saying, *My child is perfect, there is not a thing that I would change,* what might we look for inside us all during this High Holy Day period?

I would like to suggest five flaws that each one of us might be able to find within ourselves.

The first flaw we could find within ourselves I would call: *Outward Grandeur vs. Internal Emptiness.* I refer to how we project outwardly towards those around us an appearance of honor, piety, and charity when we might only putting on a mask. Jewish folklore describes this behavior as being like someone who has the key to the inner chamber of the gold depository but not the key to the outside room. To fix this flaw we must strive to improve ourselves from within.

The second flaw we might consider is: *materialism as the bread of our souls*. Instead of using what God has given us to bring bread to those less fortunate, we might sometimes only look at what our *neighbor* has and want the same. In this case we could ask ourselves what is more important; another piece of clothing, furniture or anything else we might want or helping others overcome their daily struggles.

Judaism teaches in the *Jerusalem Talmud Berachot 4: kol Yisrael arevim zeh bazeh: all Israel is responsible for one another*: *let us use the quiet meditations within our hearts these High Holy Days to ask if we are truly responsible for one another.*

In my mind the third flaw that every Jewish individual can search for deep within himself is to see where he stands religiously: *Do we confuse religious affiliations for religious beliefs?*

The fourth flaw that I often wonder about myself and our society is: *Do I/we take for granted those around us or do we work every day to make those relationships with family and friends even stronger?* How can we constantly realize how lucky we are in our daily lives to be surrounded by those who love us? Do we love back? Do we give back as we should? Do we say thank you and I love you or do we allow our own personal flaws to keep us from expressing how we truly feel?

The fifth possible flaw that I would suggest is directly related to the High Holy Days, and that is: *Do we see the High Holy Days only as an opportunity to appease our conscience or do we use these few days as an opportunity to purify our souls?* The path toward purification, in my mind, begins by looking inside ourselves and actually seeing our strengths and weaknesses, thus allowing ourselves to enhance our strengths and fight off any weakness that we may have.

If we can look within ourselves in order to change and grow, then this High Holy Day period will not only usher in a new year but will also usher in new and improved individuals.

CONFORMITY AND ABDICATION OF INDEPENDENT THINKING

In American culture people often conform to what is popular and fashionable. This conformity affects the cars and clothes we buy. It also influences, in many instances, the type of God we believe in. Our teachers pass down to us their philosophies of God, and the opinions that they state all too often are taken carte blanche for the truth.

I remember a professor in my undergraduate studies who once taught that God and religion were just creations of historical thinkers in order to control the masses. Quickly this became the position of some of the students in our class.

I also remember a very Orthodox professor in rabbinical school who taught that the *Talmud* is the pure truth and the only appropriate manifestation of God's oral law. Thus it should not be researched and critically analyzed; it should only be studied, memorized and followed.

Unfortunately this also became the opinion of some of my fellow students. This sort of thinking, whereby one relinquishes one's own ability to think independently and enter into a relationship with the text and with God, only serves to diminish one's intellectual autonomy. Furthermore it negates the fact that each and every one of us has the right and responsibility to enter into a personal dialogue with God.

This phenomenon of handing over to others how we converse with God is taking place all too frequently in Jewish communities and synagogues. I have noticed while *davening (praying)* at synagogues in Israel, England, and the United States that commentators such as *Rashi* and *Maimonides* are quoted as holding the absolute truths.

This to me is very ironic, for the multitude of commentaries, opinions and even legalistic rulings in Judaism underscores the obvious fact that we are not a one-dimensional people. We are a pluralistic and ever evolving religion.

While many of us see the fact that there are Orthodox, Conservative, Reform and other movements in Judaism as tragic; to me it is beautiful. The complexity of understandings ensures that learning and debate will continue to help us live in the present and evolve and remain relevant in the future.

The very texts that we read and disagree upon are there to make sure that we talk. I don't mean solely talking about God, but also taking the second step and talking to God.

The texts that we read are not sacred because others have told us so; rather they become truly sacred when we incorporate them into our lives. Our sacred texts become lost when we interpret our theologies solely in the realm of philosophy. While relating to our theological and religious beliefs in philosophical concepts is legitimate, and at times very stimulating, as well as a path towards God, theology is also meant to be spiritual.

I realize that it is more comfortable to rely on philosophy and scholarship when trying to understand and build a relationship with God. The search for spirituality is difficult, but it can be very rewarding and life altering.

At this point you may be saying, "I agree that it is important to enter a relationship with God on a deeper level, but I don't know where to begin." The start of such a journey may seem daunting and complex, but one way to begin on a path towards God is very simple. What is required is a reinterpretation of the word covenant.

Traditionally the term covenant can be understood as a holy relationship between man and man or man and God. In the Bible it is used mostly when speaking about the relationship between God and the *Children of Israel* or the *Children of Israel's* representatives. For example, in the beginning of the book of *Exodus* we learn about the covenant between Moses and God, which was solidified at the Burning Bush, and later between the *Children of Israel* and God at Mount Sinai when the *Ten Commandments* or *Decalogue* was given. These examples of covenants show the two-way relational moments whereby the *Children of Israel* began their journeys from the ordinary into the realm of holiness.

However the traditional definition of covenant need not be the only path by which we can enter into the realm of holiness in our connections to others as well as to God. We can look at each human relationship as being a holy covenant between people created in God's image. Furthermore my sense of covenant need not be understood as a two-way relationship between men or between man and God.

In my personal theological view (which is continuously developing), we can understand covenant as turning the ordinary into holiness. For example, if we were to look at a tree in the fall with its beautiful leaves not only as an exquisite part of nature there for us to observe, but also as a way to comprehend and see the beauty of God in all of His creations, then our relationship with the world around us would transform from the conventional into holiness.

Another example of how we can change our relationship to the world into one of covenant is by looking at the world not only as a byproduct of man's creations, but rather as it was intended to be: a representation of the uniqueness and holiness of God. In the realm of our everyday interactions with others we can also change our actions into covenant-based relationships. For example, if we see the person in the supermarket or any other workplace not only as an employee who is there to service our needs, but rather as another holy person created in God's image, then even those moments at the checkout line can become holy.

The relationship doesn't have to be mutual to be holy; it only needs to come from our own inner perception of the world around us.

When this is accomplished, we will not only be hearing God's words, we will also be talking with God. For everything around us will be seen as a representation of God. In essence, all of our conversations, whether personal or commercial in nature, will take on a component of holiness. In this holiness our covenants will become enriched.

Thus, we will not have to rely solely on our ancient commentators for our relationship with God. We will transform ourselves into modern day commentators who live in the realms of covenants and holiness. We will each leave a mark on society as significant as that left by *Rashi* or *Maimonides*. I look forward to all of us entering these covenants together.

THANKSGIVING AND PUMPKIN PIE

I can almost taste them, the turkey, pumpkin pie and hot apple cider. I'm not sure if my memories of these delicacies are as good as these foods actually taste. However the anticipation of the first bite of turkey and stuffing and the smell of the burning pinewood in the fireplace makes me yearn for Thanksgiving. I remember as a kid how my family would all gather together during those brisk November mornings in anticipation of the afternoon meal.

We would gather together in our family room and catch up on the events of the last year, and then we would huddle around the television to watch the Thanksgiving Day Parade. The colors of the floats and the excitement of what was coming down the road next always kept us riveted to the television. It did not matter what the announcers were talking about, but it was the fascination of the floats that kept us watching.

This of course was true until the really important event of the day started. That was the two NFL football games that always preceded and followed my family's dinner. It would seem that we always ate between these games. I can still see how Roger

TWO MINUTES OF TRADITIONS

Staubach would roll out left and throw a touchdown pass to beat the Detroit Lions year after year. I personally did not grow up as a Dallas Cowboys fan (yes I am rooting for them now) but the beauty of their passing and rushing games, added to always seeing Tom Landry with his hat walking around the sidelines seemed to make me a fan on that one day.

Thanksgiving is truly an American holiday. In 1621 the settlers of Plymouth gathered to give thanks to God for a bountiful harvest after their first year in America. This was a time when the settlers and the Native American Indians still cooperated. Their common goal of survival outweighed their differences of culture, religion and language.

If only this unity had lasted over the long haul we might be a better society today.

In 1789, after Congress adopted the Constitution (in my mind the second most important document in the modern free world after the *Tanach*), President George Washington proclaimed November 26th as a *Day of Thanksgiving*. In President Washington's proclamation we can see a desire to trace the newly formed United States and its people to a common past, thus uniting the country while also setting up a day which would link the beginning of the country to its future generations. Finally in 1863, President Lincoln proclaimed the last Thursday in November a national *Thanksgiving Day*, an official *American holiday*.

All this history is nice to know, but I still think that Thanksgiving has to do with family, football and floats. However putting aside my personal thoughts as well as the historical development of the holiday that we will all be celebrating in a few days, a question still remains in my mind. Where did the Pilgrims get the notion for such a holiday?

The answer is simple, it is from the holiday of *Sukkot,* and it is this connection that I would like to show you with a few specific examples of how we know that *Sukkot* is the origin of Thanksgiving. The first example will be from early pilgrim history while the rest will come directly from some of the many Jewish interpretations as to the meaning of the holiday *Sukkot.*

Many of the first Pilgrims called America the New Canaan, and gave their children such biblical names as Ezekiel, Moses, Solomon and Hannah. A Puritan minister, Cotton Mathew, spoke of the *Pilgrims as our happy Israel in America,* while William Bradford, who was the second Governor of Plymouth, was known as a new Moses. Cotton Mather himself called the early magistrates *ba'alei nefesh*, which in Hebrew means *people of purity.*

The ministers themselves were known as *Chasidim ha-rishonim,* or *first pious people.* Finally John Winthrop, who was governor of the Massachusetts colony, was called *Nehemias Americanus,* the American Nehemiah. Nehemiah being the first Jewish governor of Palestine after the Jews returned from the exile in Babylon. *(Material taken from Understanding Jewish Holidays and Customs, written by Sol Scharfstein).*

These examples themselves show how the first settlers tied most of their beginnings to the Bible, and Thanksgiving's ties to *Sukkot* was no different. To show how true this is we must ask briefly what does the holiday of *Sukkot* symbolize?

Sukkot has two names:

1. *Chag Ha-Sukkot* or *Festival of Tabernacles.*
2. *Chag Ha-Asif* or *Festival of Ingathering.*

Both of these names have unique characteristics. While each is unique, as we shall see, both can connect the modern day holiday of Thanksgiving with its Biblical predecessor *Sukkot.*

Chag Ha-Sukkot celebrates God's guarding the *Children of Israel* during their 40 years in the desert. The *Sukkah* or booth protected the Israelites from the harsh elements they encountered along their way from Egypt to Israel. In relationship to this the Thanksgiving that the pilgrims celebrated also was in recognition of their surviving that first harsh winter in the New World.

The second name for *Sukkot* is *Chag Ha-Asif,* which as we stated above celebrates the harvest of the first fruits in Palestine. This was the time that the grapes were ready to be made into wine, and the olives pressed into oil. Thanksgiving also came about to celebrate the first successful harvest of the pilgrims.

Finally *Sukkot* is one of the three pilgrimage festivals to Jerusalem. During this holiday a Jew is supposed to make the journey to Jerusalem. During the time of the temple this journey was to offer a sacrifice. Today the journey is more symbolic than anything else. However to be in Jerusalem today during *Sukkot* is also very special. For one can go to any restaurant in the city and eat in a *Sukkah*, and believe me the feeling one gets while eating such a meal is truly special. As to Thanksgiving, it too can be interpreted as a pilgrimage, a pilgrimage from the Old Country to the New Canaan as seen in the words and feelings of the Puritan Preacher Cotton Mather.

In conclusion it will be nice to know when I sit down this year in front of the turkey with the warmth of family and friends around me that my American and Jewish roots will be coming together once again. I will not only be celebrating an American tradition, but I will also be celebrating how Judaism has once again influenced the greater world in such a positive manner. *Sukkot* is a beautiful holiday and Thanksgiving has just become a little more special with my realization that it was founded on the basis of one of my personal favorite Jewish holidays.

DEVELOPMENT OF BELIEFS AND TORAH

Throughout the years, various congregational members ask me all kinds of questions. One that I hear frequently is, *Do our beliefs in the Torah change over time?* The question of the development of *Torah* is central to the beliefs of Conservative Judaism. In ancient times, once the *Torah* was written down, our sages tried to understand the literal meanings of the *Torah*. From that developed an oral law, which became written. From the *Mishnah* came the *Talmud*. The rabbis believed that the right way to eat a meal or conduct personal relationships could be found within the *Torah*.

As time passed and the Jewish people spread throughout the world, their inquiries and studies resulted in different kinds of knowledge. The fields of Jewish philosophy, *Kabbalah,* and history have all added to the Jewish traditions. Judaism has always evolved, as questions are raised and addressed. Majority opinions and minority opinions survive in print, leading to differing *minhagim* or customs.

For many Jews who practice the Orthodox tradition, certain aspects of Judaism do not change over time. Jews in the liberal tradition -- such as Conservative and

Reform -- look beyond the writings of the sages. We use the tools of modern Biblical criticism, like archeology, historical inquiry, and politics, to shed light on our interpretation of the tradition.

Did our ancient forebears expect the *Torah* to change? Let's explore some examples of texts related to this question.

In *Pirke Avot (Ethics of the Fathers)*, we read: *Moses received the Torah at Sinai and handed it down to Joshua; Joshua to the elders; the elders to the prophets; and the prophets to the Men of the Great Assembly. They (the Men of the Great Assembly) said three things: Be deliberate in judgment; raise up many students; and make a fence for the Torah.*

From this passage, I find several teachings. First, *Torah* has been transmitted from one generation to the next. The purposes of this transmission include allowing each generation to study the texts and design its own additions to the literature. Moreover, the leaders of every generation may interpret and make relevant the *Torah* for their times.

What did they mean in the phrase, *make a fence for the Torah?* To make the *Torah* understandable and accessible for today's generation, we must ensure that our interpretations serve only to preserve *Torah* and widen the belief and study of the *Torah*. While we can widen the fence when we employ the disciplines of history and archeology to study *Torah*, we must always stay within the fence. We must not use modern science to destroy belief, but rather to make our beliefs stronger and relevant to the current human condition.

The following story from the *Talmud* provides another lesson.

If the halacha agrees with me, let it be proved from heaven! Whereupon a heavenly voice cried out: "Why do you dispute with R. Eliezer seeing that in all matters of [insert word] halacha agrees with him?" But R. Joshua arose and exclaimed, "It is not in heaven!" What did he mean by this? Said R. Jeremiah; "That the Torah has already been given at Mount Sinai, therefore we pay no attention to a heavenly voice, because You have long since written in the Torah at Mount Sinai; After the majority must one incline" (Exodus 23:2). R. Nathan met Elijah and asked him: "What did the Holy One, blessed be He, do at that hour?" He replied: "He laughed, saying, My sons have defeated me, My sons have defeated me." (Babylonian Talmud Baba Mezia 59a-b)

In other words, it is for us today to decide what is Jewish law and learning. How do contemporary Conservative Jews decide what falls within the scope of *Talmud Torah* and what must remain outside of this realm? Personally when I speak of *Talmud Torah*, I am referring to both the written and oral traditions that have been passed down from generation to generation.

How do we choose what texts to study in our own personal Jewish libraries, and what materials to exclude?

Conservative Judaism uses two methods of inquiry. The first is historical: How did a tradition endowed with religious dignity come to be formed? (history, sociology, politics, etc.)

The second deals with interpretation: How was this tradition understood once it had been accepted as a religious phenomenon? Were there single interpretations or multiple meanings? In the Orthodox world once a tradition has been accepted the question of historical development of that tradition is no longer relevant. For the historian and Conservative Jew alike the historical question remains fundamental in deciding how we interpret the information.

A third example elucidates this point. It is written in the *Talmud* that women can read from the *Torah* and even serve as *Mohalim*. Nevertheless, *for the public dignity, women are forbidden.*

What does that mean? Both religious practice and social norms were oriented to men at that time. For a woman to read from *Torah*, while some men in the community were unable to read, would not look good for the whole congregation. In present times, women have become more fully integrated into all societal roles Women possess equal rights under United States law. We have in our midst almost an equal number of women and men who are *Torah* readers in today's Conservative synagogues. We cannot now argue that women may not read from the *Torah*. Therefore, the emphasis of the Conservative movement is placed on the first part of the statement, *Women can read from the Torah,* and not on the restriction that closes the passage.

If you ask me, *What is an appropriate Conservative opinion?* I have no quick or easy answer, although as I have shown our understanding of *Torah* and *halacha* is always developing. Throughout the Conservative movement, since its inception, we have grappled with these issues.

It is my hope that we will never stop striving for the answers. As we continue to grow as a learning community, Conservative Judaism will remain a vibrant and dynamic movement.

HOW DOES ISRAEL BLEND INDEPENDENCE DAY AND MEMORIAL DAY ONE AFTER THE OTHER?

After having spent 12 years in Israel, two and a half of those in the Army and numerous months in the reserves, the spring and especially the month of April makes me think of *Holocaust Memorial Day* which takes place on April 19th of this year, *Memorial Day for all fallen soldiers and those who died protecting the State of Israel*, which falls on April 25th and finally *Independence Day* which immediately follows on the 26th of April. It is specifically the question of *Memorial Day* for fallen soldiers leading directly into *Independence Day* that I would like to ponder with you.

Thinking back on the time I lived in Israel, I have three distinct memories of *Memorial Day/Independence Day*. The first memory dates back to my first year in Israel. That year while living in Jerusalem, I marked, like most other residents of Israel, *Memorial Day* by standing for a moment of national silence, visiting a military graveyard and watching TV programs about fallen soldiers and listening to the roll call of every fallen soldier's name on the state television. This memory left me with the impression that no one, not one single soldier who gave his or her life for the state would ever be forgotten. It was with this memory and the feeling that came with it that I went out later in the evening to see how most Israelis, at least in Jerusalem, made the transition from the sadness of *Memorial Day* to the joy of *Independence Day*.

Somehow I found myself in the middle of Jerusalem in Zion Square. There the sight that greeted me was incredible. For around me I saw Israelis of all ages celebrating together with such joy that I almost forgot that only a few moments earlier the whole country was in a state of mourning. I also got caught up in the joy for I felt a part of Israel and Israeli society, but I still went home pondering how I could reconcile my different emotions, sadness and joy together.

It was only during my second year in Israel, while I was already in the Army that I was able to begin to reconcile this paradox of days and feelings. During that year's celebration, 1989, I was in the army's furthermost front line artillery position inside Lebanon.

My unit, which had a great feeling of comradery and family, marked these days with a military honor guard at our base for those who had fallen during our units history. It was only then and later on in the evening when we celebrated life and freedom that I started to understand how these two totally opposite days of emotion could be celebrated one right after the other.

I finally understood that *Independence Day* was another way of honoring the greatest sacrifice that those defenders of the State of Israel and their families had made. *Independence Day* was a celebration about freedom, a freedom which those soldiers who we mourned just a few hours before, had helped to preserve. I at that moment, was a direct link to those who had fallen as well as to those who had survived and continued to ensure that Israel would always remain free.

This feeling followed me for a few years until tragedy hit a close friend of mine and his family. While living on a Kibbutz, outside Tel Aviv, my best friend at that time, who had arranged for me to come and live on the Kibbutz lost his brother during a training mission in one of Israel's most elite forces.

I remember vividly the moment I was notified and told Michal and how we went together to visit my friend and his family.

Needless to say they were devastated, and remain so. During the next *Memorial Day/Independence Day* I saw that my friend had no happiness but only sorrow both during *Memorial Day* and *Independence Day*. It was at this point that I realized that the families who had lost a loved one did not feel as I felt only a few years earlier since my time in the army, and this made me rethink my own view and feelings on the close proximity of these days.

While I have not found an answer that totally satisfies my feelings, my studies of different Jewish texts has led me to some conclusions on the subject of sacrifice for the sake of freedom.

In the Bible we learn that the *Children of Israel* are commanded to go to war against their biblical enemy *Amalek* who attacked the *Children of Israel* right after they had left Egypt. Due to this attack we read, *the Lord will have war with Amalek from generation to generation. (Exodus 17:16)*

What does this mean? To me it means that the *Children of Israel*, with God by their side, shall always fight against enemies who seek to destroy her, thus ensuring her survival but at the same time tragically losing some of those same individuals who helped to ensure that survival. Thus already we see in the Bible that freedom comes often at a very costly price. However, for us not to think that the *Children of Israel* is a nation who automatically goes to war to ensure its survival, we must look at some of the *Mishnaic* literature which was codified around the year 200 C.E.

In this literature, which serves as the basis for Jewish law, we read that the Israelites must offer terms of peace before they go to war. How can we interpret this fact? Here we must conclude that independence, which can be maintained and fortified without bloodshed, is always preferable to warfare itself. However, when the *Torah* itself and thus the *Children of Israel* are directly in danger *all go forth, even a bridegroom from his chamber and a bride from her canopy (Babylonian Talmud, Sotah 44b).* Unfortunately this has been and continues to be the situation in Israel today. Thus Israel still needs a strong military to fend off her modern day enemies, just as she needed one to defend herself from her biblical enemy, *Amalek.*

This knowledge combined with my own experiences has led me to conclude that our independence will always be tied to the sacrifice that we as a Jewish people have had to make along the way. While this does not totally comfort me or allow me to be overly joyous on *Independence Day,* as I am sure that it does not comfort those families that have lost their loved ones it does make me understand the logic of the leaders of Israel who decided to intertwine *Memorial* and *Independence* days together.

Let us hope and pray that this upcoming year and years to come Israel should not lose anyone else in her fight for independence and that *nation shall not lift up sword against nation, neither shall they learn war any more (Isaiah 2:4).* It is with this hope that I shall mark both *Memorial Day* and *Independence Day* later this month.

SCHOOL'S OUT!

These two words often cause different reactions from several groups of people. They can stimulate trepidation for parents who now have to figure out what to do with their children during the summer. The possibilities are many: family vacations, summer employment, day camps, sleep-away camps, the pool, and friends' sleepovers and so on. When I was a child, my parents sent my sister and me to Camp Ramah and later to Camp Tel Shalom.

For kids these two words often symbolize freedom. They have been counting down since early spring until the emancipation from homework, teachers, and all the subjects they have been complaining about. For teachers the words *School's Out* also connect to a feeling of freedom. They no longer have to prepare daily lesson plans or commute to school or prepare reports that take time from the true purpose of school, teaching and learning. For another group the words *School's Out* means summer vacation and economic prosperity. Many camps, activities and trips are run specifically during the summer break.

School's Out has aroused my curiosity about what Jewish sources say about school or *Bet Midrash (house of study).* One of the earliest references to a *Bet Midrash* can be found in a *Midrash* concerning Jacob and Esau. *Rabbi Phinehas said in Rabbi Levi's name: They were like a myrtle and a wild rose bush growing side by side; when they attained to maturity, one yielded its fragrance and the other its thorns. So for thirteen years both went to school and came home from school. After this age, one went to the house of study and the other to idolatrous shrines (Genesis Rabba 63:10).*

The surface meaning is that both Jacob and Esau studied until the age of 13, and afterwards only one continued in the study of *Torah* while the other left his studies and came under the influence of idolatry. However underneath this simple explanation, the text is trying to teach us something of greater importance. A formal education is not enough. One must also have a love of learning and a willingness to study in order to reap the greatest benefits. This source also teaches us that learning must never stop, *school is never out*, for if we stop learning as individuals we might get involved in negative activities just as Esau got caught up with idolatry.

The importance of the *Bet Midrash* became even more evident during the period when the *Talmud* was written (200-500 C.E.). There we read, *A scholar should not reside in a city where the following ten things are not found: a court of justice that imposes flagellation and decrees penalties; a charity fund collected by two and distributed by three; a*

Synagogue; public baths; toilet facilities; a circumciser; a surgeon; a notary; a slaughterer; and a school-master (Sanhedrin 17b).

This Talmudic passage sets up a guideline for a proper city, one that contains institutions that tend to the spiritual, hygienic, health, religious and educational needs of all its citizens. The schoolmaster being listed shows to me the importance that education was given in Jewish communities.

We know of other Talmudic passages that praise women for insuring the education of their children and husbands. *Wherewith do women acquire merit? By making their children learn at the synagogue and their husbands study at the college and by waiting for their husbands till they return from the college (Berakhot 17a).* Thus a wife or mother is rewarded for her active support and indirect participation in the pursuit of knowledge by her family members. Although *Bet Midrash* for children is not mentioned we can infer from later commentators that within many synagogues schools of education could be found.

We have seen that a city will only be blessed with scholars if a schoolmaster lives there and that a mother is rewarded for sending her husband and children to school. However all of these rewards deal with the here and now, and if we look hard enough we can also find that education is rewarded in the world to come. In a *Midrash* on *Parshat Ki Tavo from the book of Deuteronomy*, Rabbi Joshua ben Levi said:

Whosoever enters synagogues and houses of study in this world will be privileged to enter synagogues and houses of study in the time to come. Whence this? For it is said 'Happy are they that dwell in Thy house, they will for ever praise Thee' (Psalms 84:5). Moses said to Israel: "Since whosoever listens to the words of the Torah is so exalted in both worlds..." (Deuteronomy Rabba 7:1).

Here we see that learning in the house of study in general and the learning of *Torah* in particular (which took place in the house of study) was guaranteed to continue in the world to come. Studying is a lifelong pursuit and not just something we do ten months of the year.

We also read, *Rabbi Levi ben Hiyya said: One who on leaving the synagogue goes into the house of study and studies the Torah is deemed worthy to welcome the Divine Presence, as it says, They go from strength to strength, every one of them appeareth before God in Zion" (Berakhot 64a).* The inference here is that a house of study or *Bet Midrash* is considered *strength* alongside another important and central Jewish institution, the synagogue.

Once again study in this world will ensure our continuous development in the world to come.

References to the importance of education can be found in current literature. The late great Rabbi Abraham Joshua Heschel once said, *When I pray I speak to God and when I study God speaks to me.* Our continuous striving for knowledge enables God to speak to us through the traditions that we are studying. Prayer and study create a personal dialogue with God while ensuring that this dialogue will continue through the teachings we pass on to our children.

As we have seen, even though *SCHOOL'S OUT,* it really never ends. We might presently be preparing for the months of June, July and August. But our quest for knowledge must never end. In the end learning never stops in this world or in the world to come.

THE SINS OF OUR POLITICAL LEADERS

I am personally both disheartened and tired of the wrongdoing that our *leaders* have done. The *Torah* teaches what the leader should do when the offense is made public: *In case it is a chieftain who incurs guilt by doing unwittingly any of the things which by the commandment of the Lord his God ought not to be done, and he realizes his guilt – or the sin of which he is guilty is brought to his knowledge – he shall bring as his offering a male goat without blemish (Leviticus 4:22-23).*

Having grown up in America, and having spent twelve years in Israel, I am afraid that some of our recent *chieftains* never learned these verses. First we had President Nixon and the Watergate scandal that led to his resignation from office. More recently, we saw the former Governor Blagojevich of Illinois, who is now sitting in jail for influence peddling and bribery. In Israel, former President Ezer Weizman was charged with bribery and influence peddling and resigned. Arie Deri, leader of the Ultra Orthodox Shas Party, was convicted and imprisoned for bribery and former President, Moshe Katzav is now sitting in jail for sexual offences perpetrated against a number of young women who served under him. None of these people made a formal acknowledgment of their wrongdoing.

Did these leaders not know that they were sinning? Perhaps their official powers and feelings of superiority blinded them to the truth that all people must obey the law. We are told over and over again during the High Holiday season (which is just around the corner) that our actions, both between God and us and between other people and us must be moral in their character. The behavior of these leaders is not acceptable today and has never been acceptable among the Children of Israel. For when a ruler has sinned even unknowingly, he must offer a sacrifice and make atonement.

Has *Am Yisrael* maintained this strict level of morality throughout the ages, or has the law remained on the books while not being practiced in reality? To answer such a question one may look in the *Talmud* and study the actions and teachings of one of *Am Yisrael's* great rabbinic sages, Rabbi Johanan ben Zakkai. His story became the foundation for subsequent Jewish law.

In the *Babylonian Talmud* we read: *Rabbi Johanan ben Zakkai said: Happy is the generation whose ruler brings a sacrifice for a sin he has committed unwillingly. If its ruler brings a sacrifice, is there any need to say what one of the common people would do: and if he brings a sacrifice for a sin he has committed unwillingly, is there any need to say what he would do in case of a sin committed willfully? (Babylonian Talmud Masechet Horayoth 10b)*

In this passage Rabbi Johanan ben Zakkai is praising a generation due to the actions of its rulers. *Happy is the generation*: Why is the generation happy, one could ask? Is it because the ruler acts in the same manner that he demands from his people? Is it because both the ruler and his people are equal in God's eyes? Is it possibly because the *ruler* in this case sets a personal example for his people? Maybe the generation would be *happy* because they would now have a ruler who would be to his people a moral compass upon which they could direct their own lives. In the end, I think all three of these reasons were true. A ruler with a high level of morality is one that always makes his people strive to be better themselves.

Were these merely the words of a moral Rabbi, or were they also the teachings he himself followed? If Rabbi Johanan ben Zakkai also lived by the Bible's teachings that he himself taught *(that we quoted from Leviticus 4:22-23)*, we will see that this sage of Rabbinic Judaism called for a higher quality of leadership than we find in some of our modern day politicians.

In the *Babylonian Talmud, Masechet Bearchoth* we read: *When Rabban (Rabbi) Johanan ben Zakkai fell ill, his disciples went in to visit him. When he saw them he began to weep. His disciples said to him: Lamp of Israel, pillar of the right hand, mighty hammer! Wherefore weepest thou? He replied: If I were being taken today before a human king who is here today and tomorrow in the grave, whose anger if he is angry with me does not last for ever, who if he imprisons me does not imprison me forever and who if he puts me to death does not put me to everlasting death, and whom I can persuade with words and bribe with money, even so I would weep. Now that I am being taken before the supreme King of Kings, the Holy One, blessed be He, who lives and endures for ever and ever whose anger, if He is angry with me, is an everlasting anger, who if He imprisons me imprisons me forever, who if He puts me to death puts me to death forever, and who I cannot persuade with words or bribe with money -- nay more, when there are two ways before me, one leading to Paradise and the other to Gehinnom, and I do not know by which I shall be taken, shall I not weep?"* (Babylonian Talmud Maechet Berachoth 28b)

What does this scene between Rabbi Johanan ben Zakkai and his students teach us? Many scholars think that it relates to the famous story of his escape from Jerusalem and his negotiations with the Romans for *Yavneh and its Sages.* According to these scholars, Rabbi Johanan ben Zakkai did not know if he had transgressed in his actions. On his deathbed he was still trying to figure out if he had done the right thing.

I believe, historically speaking, it is safe to say from the development of Rabbinic Judaism that Rabbi Johanan ben Zakkai made the right choice. However, I think that this story has something much more basic to teach us, something that ties in with the *High Holy Days.* When it comes to morality there is only one course: one that helps all mankind uphold the standard by which we all were created. Was not man *created in Gods image?* When a *ruler* who has sinned makes an *offering,* that shows the true leader is one who chooses the path that leads to Paradise, and not the road that leads to Gehinnom.

We can all learn from the example of Rabbi Johanan ben Zakkai. The only way to act is by making amends for our sins. While today we don't make animal sacrifices by which we can atone for our sins, I have no doubt that each and every one of us can find a way to make our own personal offerings of peace to whomever we might have hurt, either intentionally or unintentionally during this upcoming *High Holy Day season.* I only wish our politicians and society as a whole would be quicker to learn this lesson.

ELIE WIESEL

I have always loved to read auto-biographies. The latest book in this genre I have been reading is Elie Wiesel's memoir, *And the Sea Is Never Full*. This book blends his perspectives on modern history, personal journeys, and religious beliefs. Wiesel writes about the importance of a nation's collective memory. A nation must remember all of its historical, cultural, religious and moral foundations while reinterpreting them for the present.

Remembering and honoring the collective history of the *Children of Israel* is one of two important reasons we have survived for thousands of years. The other is the reinterpretation of our biblical past.

Let us take the story of Abraham as an example. In the *Book of Genesis, Parshat Lekh L'kha,* we read that God commands Abram (his original name) to *go forth from your native land and from your father's house to the land that I will show you (Gen. 12: 1-2).*

Abram is ordered to leave his home without being told why. Later in the *Parsha (Gen. 17:5)* we read that God changes Abram's name to Abraham by adding the letter *hey* to the spelling. The *hey* signifies God's name and His covenant with Abraham. However, we are never told why God specifically selects Abraham.

A later *Midrash* offers an explanation of why Abraham was chosen. The story tells us that Abraham's father Terah, who owned an idol shop, once went on a journey and left Abraham in charge. The *Talmud* relates to us the following episode. *A woman came and placed before the idols in the shop a bowl of flour as a sacrificial offering. No sooner had the woman left than Abraham picked up a stick and broke all the idols. Only one, the largest, did he spare. In the hand of this one Abraham then placed the stick.*

Upon his return Terah saw the destruction Abraham had wrought among the idols. He flung himself upon him crying, "Who did this?"

"Just listen father and be amazed!" replied Abraham serenely. 'A woman came and brought a full bowl of flour for an offering. I placed the bowl at the feet of the idols. Immediately, a murderous battle broke out among them. Each of the idols said the flour was meant for him. While they all squabbled and pulled, the largest of them, determined to create order, picked up a stick and said, '...See for yourself -- he killed them all!'

You ne'er-do-well! cried Abraham's father. How can you say the idols squabbled and pulled when they can neither speak nor understand? "Father, father!" replied Abraham, "the holy truth lies in your words!"

Abraham deserved to be the first person to enter a new covenant with God because he understood that idols were only inanimate objects that held no real power, in comparison to the God of Abraham whose power was infinite and not dependent on any physical form. In this realization and through his actions Abraham became the first monotheist.

How is this story relevant for us? There are many kinds of idols today. Some would point to the use of dishonest and immoral business practices used to gain material wealth for oneself at the expense of other employees, investors, or others. In the Enron scandal we saw how some of the executives cheated the company in order to enrich themselves. The pursuit of unending wealth became their god. This idolatry ultimately led to thousands of individuals losing their future livelihoods and retirement pensions.

Another example of modern idolatry is a person's total assimilation into the dominant American culture and the loss of a Jewish identity. There are Jews who become anti-Semites to be accepted. I went through high school in rural Maryland with such an individual. A Jewish student played on the football team. To be totally accepted in his teammate's eyes, the young man not only cast off any outward symbols or pride in his Judaism, but he also verbally and physically tormented the few other Jews at school. His own self-hatred and desire to be accepted became his false god.

We might also recognize as idolatry some of the cult-like status given to sports and entertainment figures. Too often we try to follow the latest "thing," at the expense of our own identity. Lady Gaga may be appealing, but we don't need our kids trying to become her. There are many famous personalities who may be talented in their respective fields, but we don't need to accept their political opinions because they are famous. The idolatry here is the worshipping of famous people at the loss of our own opinions and individuality.

The message that we can take from the Abraham story and apply to our own lives is that our belief in God must be our true ultimate value.

As a community, when we pray or study, or whenever and wherever we meet, let us continue to remember and apply the foundation of our collective identity. I look forward to taking this journey with you.

TWO MINUTES OF TRADITIONS

ENTERING INTO A RELATIONSHIP WITH GOD

I was reading a book the other day when I came across an interesting *Midrash* about a man named Sam. The *Midrash* states that *As Sam was reading the biography of a medieval Rabbi, he felt a growing irritation. Though he thought that the book was worthwhile, the biographer kept invoking God in the text, and Sam felt these references were a major obstacle to his understanding the Rabbi's life.*

He decided that since he didn't know what God meant, he would substitute 'X' in his mind whenever he came across the term, thereby reminding himself that he didn't know how the author was using the word. Finally, when he had finished reading the book, he realized that only then did he know what God meant to the author and to the Rabbi.

Furthermore Sam realized that the commandment *You shall not take the name of Adonai your God in vain,* was meant to prohibit man from allowing God's name to be historically misused, coerced, and fanaticized so that the true meaning of God would never actually come to the surface.

Sam realized that it takes an enormous effort to suspend judgment and discover what God's name truly means. In today's society we are, unfortunately, not very similar to Sam in his way of thinking.

In the modern culture that we live in we all too often conform to what is popular and fashionable. This sort of thinking, in actuality negates our own intellectual autonomy. Instead of thinking independently, we all too often tend to follow the norm, no matter whether that norm is healthy or not for us as individuals.

The problematic truth of this statement is even more magnified when our loss of independent thinking transcends the realm of cultural comforts and enters the realm of intellectual honesty. Unfortunately this phenomenon is also taking place in the realm of religion. For each religion has its own writings and interpretations that are taught as the absolute truth rather than the individual perspective of the commentator who was trying to understand the same texts as we do.

I have prayed at synagogues in Israel, England, and in the United States, and in many of them *Rashi*, *Maimonides* and in modern times *Hertz* are quoted as holding the absolute truths. The fact that this takes place is very ironic in my eyes, for the multitude of commentaries, opinions and even legalistic rulings in Judaism underscores that we are not a one dimensional people, rather we are a pluralistic evolving religion.

While to many the fact that there are Orthodox, Conservative, Reform and other movements in Judaism is tragic, for me it is beautiful. The complexity of understandings ensures that learning and debate will continue to help us not only to live in the present but also ensures that we evolve and remain relevant in the future.

The very texts that we read and disagree upon are there to make sure that we talk. I don't mean talking about God, but more importantly, talking to God. The texts that we read are not sacred because others have told us so; rather they become sacred when we incorporate them into our lives. Our sacred texts become lost when we interpret our theologies solely into the realm of philosophy. Theology is meant to be spiritual as well.

The scholars of our past have taught us that God speaks to us and the one who understands Him is a *talmid hacham (wise student)*. While learning in and of itself is special and important, learning to hear God is not enough. The next step must also be taken, and that is using the texts not only to hear the voice of God but also to talk with God.

The intellectual understanding of God, which our commentators try to pass on to us, should not negate the personal relationship that we need to formulate with God. I realize that it is much easier to be passive in our learning than it is to be active in our search for a relationship, but the search itself, while tough, is truly rewarding.

At this point you may be saying, *I agree that it is important to enter a relationship with God, but I don't know where to begin.*

The start of such a journey may sometimes seem very daunting and complex, but in all reality the way of beginning such a path toward God is very simple. The only thing that is required is an understanding of the word, *covenant*.

Now, let us all go forward and find out how we define and enter our covenant with God.

TWO MINUTES OF TRADITIONS

SHABBAT EVENINGS

Shabbat Evenings are always particularly special to me. Not only as a Jew who comes together Sabbath, but also as a father to young children.

Every Friday evening my family and I gather around the Shabbat table and the first thing my wife and I do is bless Daniel, Maya and Lia. The blessing, while being very personal in meaning to every parent, is at the same time standard to all who bless their children.

God make you as Ephraim and Manasseh. The Lord bless you and protect you, the Lord make His face to shine upon you, and be gracious to you: the Lord turn His face to you and give you peace.

This very meaningful blessing finds its origin in this week's *Parsha*. *And he* with his community to celebrate the start of the *blessed them that day, saying, 'By you shall Yisrael bless, saying, God make thee as Ephraim and Manasseh.' (Genesis 48:20)*. The whole story of how Ephraim and Manasseh received their blessings from Yaakov is very interesting as it is not what we might have expected. We may question that since Manasseh was the older of the two children, why was Ephraim blessed first and with Yaakov's right hand? Should not the first blessing be connected with

Manasseh's birthright? Was it possible that there was such a fundamental difference between the two brothers that the younger was blessed before his elder brother?

The bible itself does not offer an answer to this question; therefore, we must look elsewhere. The *Midrash*, as it often does, helps us to understand this story better by describing in detail both Ephraim and Manasseh's personalities. Ephraim is described as humble, someone who would always stay near his tent. In other words he was a student, a man who would spend his day studying Torah.

On the other hand Manasseh was a man of the world who would often accompany his father in his business travels. Was this the significant difference between the two – that learning is more important than work? Although we know of many who might think this to be true, we are taught that learning and work can't survive without the other.

In *The Ethics of our Fathers* we are taught the following. *Where there is no flour (bread), there is no Torah; where there is no Torah, there is no flour (bread) (Pirke Avot 3:21).*

The analogy here, according to some commentators, is that there must be an ample amount of time for both work – the flour, and study – the *Torah*. Someone who only studies will not have the physical or economic capabilities to survive, for one must also eat. And the opposite is also true. The person who only works and worries about his or her physical needs will not have the spiritual nourishment to continue on during the harshest of times.

These are two different sides of a coin, with each being equally important. Neither by themselves has any value or meaning, but bound together you receive something of true value. Having realized that both work and study are important to one's soul, and assuming therefore both Ephraim and Manasseh should have been of equal standing, I am still perplexed by the fact that Ephraim was blessed first. However there is another peculiar fact in this story and that peculiarity can be found in *Rashi's* commentary on the verse *And it came to pass after these things, that one told Yosef, Behold, your father is sick (48:1).*

Rashi here noticed that verse 1 of chapter 48 did not tell us who told Yosef that his father was ill. *Rashi* having realized this then relates to us the tradition that it was Ephraim who told Yosef that Yaakov was ill. And how did Ephraim know this? The answer to this also, according to *Rashi,* is that Ephraim used to study *Torah* with Yaakov.

So therefore he knew exactly what Yaakov's health was while Yosef and Manasseh who were businessmen of the world were less well informed. However once again can we honestly say that due to the fact that one was a student and therefore in close proximity to his grandfather that he is more preferable than his brother?

In the time of the Bible as well as today one's status was not decided solely on one's personal relationship with a parent. One's morals, the honor one affords his elders, and the general character of an individual were and still are the main factors of how well someone is respected.

A person's general character and not any one particular side of one's personality is how a person is judged by his fellow peers.

I think that this is what this week's *Parsha* is trying to teach us. The message here is not one of the scholar being more important than the worker, it is not about one grandson spending more time with his grandfather than the other, it is about two sides coming together to make a whole.

For as *Pirke Avot* teaches us, one without the other cannot survive. Ephraim without his brother Manasseh is not a complete person, and the opposite is also true. They need each other to complement each individual's character and strengths. Together they are both the *Torah* and the flour that the *Mishnah* in *Avot 3:21* talks about. So we now know why each Friday evening we bless our son as *Ephraim and Manasseh;* for only if he exhibits both of these characters will he grow up to be a complete person. This feeling of wholeness and not the sibling rivalry that we might read into the story of Ephraim and Manasseh, is the true lesson that the Torah comes to teach us this week.

AL CHET AND THE SIN OF SLANDER

I hope everyone had meaningful High Holy Days. I am editing my Yom Kippur sermon into a newsletter article per the request of a number of congregants. I hope it can be used as a guide for the upcoming year.

There is a story about a professor at the Jewish Theological Seminary who once came home after officiating at a synagogue during the High Holy Days and said to his teacher, Rabbi Simon Greenberg, *Professor Greenberg, I simply can't take the Al Chet anymore! Forty four sins repeated nine times – it's just too much!*

And Prof. Greenberg replied: *Of course it is! I haven't said them all for years.*

The professor was taken aback. *Could it be that his teacher, who was such a genuinely pious person, had not recited the Al Chet in years?* he asked.

It's very simple, said Prof. Greenberg. *Each time I choose one of the sins on the list, one that applies to me, I think about its implications and meditate on how and why I committed it – and by the time I am finished thinking about that one sin, the rest of the people have finished the whole list. (Rabbi Jack Riemer, The World of the High Holy Days, Miami, 1991, p. 301)*

In reality this is very insightful, for Jewish law requires us to confess our sins at every service on *Yom Kippur (Yoma 87B)*, but we are not required to say the exact list of *Al Chet*, which has grown steadily longer throughout the centuries. For us here today, let us look at the *Al Chet* phrases connected to speech.

For the sin we have committed before You by the utterance of our lips.

For the sin we have committed before You by slander.

And for the sin we have committed before You by tale bearing and gossip.

The first verse is a general confession of our mouth's ability to sin, but the last two verses refer to two specific commandments mentioned numerous times in the *Bible* and *Talmud* and codified by *Maimonides*. These are the sins of gossip and slander.

In the *Book of Leviticus (19:16)* we read *Do not go about as a talebearer (rachil) among your countrymen ... I am the Lord.*

What exactly is a *rachil*, a talebearer? *Rashi* writes that it comes from the word *rochel* or peddler. Just as a peddler peddles merchandise from one house to another, so a talebearer or gossip carries overheard information from one person to another. *Rambam, Hilkhot Deot 7:2*. The only difference is that a peddler has wares to sell, while a gossip only sells evil and hate.

Would you want to be in the vicinity of such a person? Could you respect such a person? I know that I would not and could not, and while we may smile on the outside to the gossiper among us, our true selves know what these individuals actually represent. Who are they fooling other than themselves?

In the *Book of Proverbs (10:18)* we read that *He who spreads slander is a fool.*

This sentiment is even expanded upon with God saying *Whoever tells lashon hara, ... 'He and I cannot inhabit the same world' (Arakhin 15b),* and *Whoever slanders has no place in the world to come. (Pirkei Derabi Eliezer 53, fol. 127a).*

Even a great man like Moses was not allowed to enter the *Promised Land* because, according to Rabbi Simone, he was not punished for striking the rock, but rather because he called the Jewish people *hamorium, rebels.* Moshe was severely punished for speaking *lashon hara* against the Jewish people (*Shir Hashirim Rabbah*).

Another rabbinic dictum takes this analogy with murder one step further: *A person who slanders, kills three – the teller, the listener, and victim (Midrash Tehillim 52).*

The devastating power of our tongues was illustrated

in Israel with the 1995 murder of then Prime Minister Yitzhak Rabin who was called a *traitor* and murdered because Yagil Amir actually believed the rhetoric he was hearing.

Lastly, *lashon hara* ultimately serves no purpose. The slanderer has harmed his victim but gained nothing in return. That is why the *Talmud* compares a slanderer to a poisonous snake – it kills others with its bite but derives no benefit from that act *(Arakhin 15b)*. A one-way poisonous relationship with a gossip or talebearer is not something to be embraced, rather it should be avoided.

So now that we know what our sources say about slanderers and gossips and why we should stay away from them, the question is how should we act? The answer here can be found in *Psalm 34*, which is recited every *Shabbat*. In it we read the words, *Who is the man who desires life, who desires years of good fortune? Guard your tongue from evil and your lips from deceitful speech.*

Let us use this upcoming year to guard our lips from evil, and only open them when we have words of praise and tribute for those around us, thus helping to ensure that we become a better society.

TORAH, EVOLUTION AND SHAVOUT
HOW DO THEY ALL GO TOGETHER?

The Holiday of *Shavuot*, which we celebrated about two weeks ago, marks the day when the Children of Israel received the *Torah*. In the *Torah Parsha,* from which we read, we hear of the thrilling events, drama and special effects that surrounded Moses ascending and descending from Mt. Sinai. Further into this *Parsha*, we read the epitome of Judaism—the *Ten Commandments*.

In the Commandment concerning keeping the Sabbath Holy, we read that we *shall not work on the seventh day, for God created the world in six days and on the seventh He rested.* It is this statement, which has always bothered me and especially bothers me during the weeks preceding *Shavuot*, when we are taught about the giving of the *Torah*, and reminded how the world was created!

You might be asking about now, *what bothers him?* My answer is the question of the world really being created in six days. For as a modern member of society, I also accept the truths of science and understand, even agree, with many of the principles in the *Theory of Evolution*. It would seem that the two contradict one another. Either Science is correct and the *Torah* is wrong, or the *Torah* is correct and Science is wrong. It doesn't seem that there is any possibility that they can be congruent.

This controversy of creationism verses Darwinism (Evolution) is not a new one. In 1925 John Thomas Scopes was arrested for teaching the theory of evolution in Dayton, Tennessee. Scopes was vilified by William Jennings Bryan who claimed that the *Torah* was the true Teaching in connection to creation.

Well in my own small way, I would like to try and synthesize the two together (*Torah and Evolution*) so we can truly be able to believe in the *Torah*, while remaining true to our understanding and acceptance of modern science. Let us look at the Torah first.

The *Torah* tells us the story of creation in a gradual manner. First we read of light and darkness. Then we read of sky and the water, and things eventually build up to the creation of animals that culminates with the creation of Man.

In essence, we see gradual stages of creation. Not everything was created at once and Man (the highest form of creation) was only created at the very end of the process, as the culmination of everything that had come before him.

Now let us look at Evolution, which can be defined as the result of numerous changes in the molecular structure of all forms of life. This adaptation, beginning with a mixture of atoms and up until this point culminating with man being the highest species of life form which we know of today. This was always shown through Evolution of the Tree of Life (picture of Apes) that many of us grew up seeing in our secular schools.

Now since it seems possible that these two very different realms of belief don't contradict each other in evolutional development, we are left with only one problem, that being the problem of time.

The *Torah* says six days, while science says millions of years. However, this is easily solved as well. We know that time in the *Torah* is not as we understand it today, a day is not necessarily 24 hours, and a year is not necessarily a 365 days (we are told that Noah lived to be 950 years old).

If this is true, and if a day just represents a unit of time (unknown in length), then we can say that the development is similar both in structure (man being last) and in time.

And if this is true: I can celebrate both *Shavuot* and Science, side by side, without any contradiction.

ABOUT THE AUTHOR

Rabbi Andrew Bloom

Rabbi Andrew Bloom was born in New Jersey, grew up in Maryland, and made aliyah at the age of 19 to Israel. There, Rabbi Bloom served for 2½ years in the Israeli Army as a combat medic in an artillery unit, and was honorably discharged in 1991 at the rank of Sergeant.

Rabbi Bloom studied education and history at the State Teachers College — Seminar Hakibutzim and Rabbinical School at The Schechter Institute for Judaic Studies in Jerusalem. Rabbi Bloom also served as a crisis counselor for English speakers at Shaarey Tzedek hospital in Jerusalem. Rabbi Bloom has served congregations in Israel, England, New Jersey and Fort Worth, Texas.

He currently serves on the Fort Worth Mayor's Faith Based Cabinet, the Fort Worth City of Compassion Steering Committee and is sought after as a lecturer on Judaism and religion within the wider communities.

He is currently serving as a resource and teacher on the internet where he reaches out to all who want to learn. His students can be found all over the world. He believes that education should not be confined to physical structures but rather should be accessible to any and every individual no matter where they may be located or their level of knowledge. This book is an outgrowth of those beliefs and his internet writings.

Rabbi Bloom firmly believes that his greatest accomplishment in life is marrying his wife Michal, and the birth of his three children, Daniel, Maya and Lia.

Made in the USA
San Bernardino, CA
27 April 2015